PRAISE FOR *Stirring the Mud*

On Swamps, Bogs, and Human Imagination

"Hurd is a consummate naturalist, writing with the grace and precision of a Peter Matthiessen or an Annie Dillard, but she is also remarkably curious about human nature, spinning her discussion to bring in Joseph Campbell, the I Ching, and Thomas Edison."
— *Los Angeles Times*

"The essays have deep reach. Like all the best such works (Annie Dillard, David Quammen and, of course, Thoreau), they make you reassess the way you look at something you thought was familiar."
— *Toronto Globe and Mail*

"Delving into these wetlands, she finds in their array of strange fauna and flora an objective correlative to the place in the mind where artistic inspiration occurs: a place of blurred borders, shifting identity, and strange odors, of rot and death, of Zen peacefulness." — *New Yorker*

"But *Stirring the Mud* is not just — even primarily — a natural history. It's about swamps as springboard for the imagination, inviting meditations on the nature of our lives." — *The Sun*

"Hurd's poetic inquiry into the life and margins of marshy terrain takes us on a magic-filled metaphorical mystery tour of human desire." — *Utne Reader*

"Barbara Hurd writes about people with the canny poise of Cheever, and about nature with the loving exactitude of Thoreau. And everywhere in her work is a speculative energy and elegance that make her essays a rare achievement." — J. D. MCCLATCHY

"Hurd's essays reverberate with an intimate, reverent understanding of nature, history, and art. The bog — metaphoric, historic, actual — has its large life here, in a book that is gracefully written and fully imagined." — JANE BROX

"This engaging book takes us deep into the swamp, both into the physical place and into its literary and mythic dimensions. *Stirring the Mud* is a smart, singular enchantment." — MARK DOTY

PRAISE FOR *Entering the Stone*
On Caves and Feeling through the Dark

"Reading *Entering the Stone* is not unlike exploring a cave system. The layout may be unclear. Some quarters may be confined. But then, unexpectedly, a seemingly unconnected chamber will converge with other passages and you find yourself in an expansive space and feel you've encountered something enlightening." — *New York Times Book Review*

"This is not a sensationalist adventure story but rather a sometimes mystical journey of discovery into the hidden recesses of the mind."
— *Library Journal*

"[An] exquisite meditation on caves and their peculiar power. . . . While plenty of writers have navigated this territory before, *Entering the Stone* seems destined to stand out among books on spelunking. There is a natural link between caves and the stalactite-covered hollows of the human heart, which Hurd plays up with elegant restraint."
— *Seattle Post-Intelligencer*

"Hurd describes not only her initiation into the stony earth but also the full range of human depths. Geology and spiritual discovery in this book are one, the evolution of Hurd's knowledge of stalactites and sightless cave fish inseparable from her encounter with fear and mystery, invisibility and intimacy, Eros and grief, life and death. *Entering the Stone* is a masterpiece of the interior world."
— JANE HIRSHFIELD

"Using a venerable literary device, Hurd explores her inner life through her fascination with caving. Her meditative, flowing prose pauses on sundry people and events in her life, which she illuminates through descriptions and comparisons with her physical surroundings in the subterranean world." — *Booklist*

"An often unnerving exploration of stone . . . A wild cave is an inscrutable space, writes Hurd, heavily symbolic, weirdly inhabited, full of squirmings. You can't see what you feel, but you sure can feel it. . . . Hurd knows she'll never understand the exact source of a cave's power, but the underground works for her." — *Kirkus Reviews*

Walking the Wrack Line

Walking the Wrack Line

On Tidal Shifts and What Remains

BARBARA HURD

THE UNIVERSITY OF GEORGIA PRESS ❧ *Athens*

Published by the University of Georgia Press
Athens, Georgia 30602
© 2008 by Barbara Hurd
All rights reserved
Designed by Walton Harris
Set in Minion Pro
Printed and bound by Maple-Vail

The paper in this book meets the guidelines for permanence
and durability of the Committee on Production Guidelines for
Book Longevity of the Council on Library Resources.

Printed in the United States of America
12   11   10   09   08   C   5   4   3   2   1

Library of Congress Cataloging-in-Publication Data

Hurd, Barbara.
Walking the wrack line : on tidal shifts and what remains /
Barbara Hurd.
       p.   cm.
ISBN-13: 978-0-8203-3102-7 (hardcover : alk. paper)
ISBN-10: 0-8203-3102-3 (hardcover : alk. paper)
1. Hurd, Barbara. I. Title.
PS3608.U766 Z477 2008
814'.6 — dc22   2007038911

Excerpt from "The Angry Winter" in *The Unexpected Universe*, © 1968
by Loren Eiseley and renewed 1996 by John A. Eichman III, reprinted by
permission of Harcourt, Inc.

Six lines of "The Stone of Heaven" used as an epigraph, from *The October
Palace* by Jane Hirshfield. © 1994 by Jane Hirshfield. Reprinted by permission
of HarperCollins Publishers.

Four lines of "Description" used as an epigraph, from *Atlantis* by Mark Doty.
© 1995 Mark Doty. Reprinted by permission of HarperCollins Publishers.

Three lines of "On the Beach" used as an epigraph, from *The Lives of the Heart*
by Jane Hirshfield. © 1997 by Jane Hirshfield. Reprinted by permission of
HarperCollins Publishers.

Publication of this book was made possible, in part, by a generous gift from Archie H. Davis in honor of Craig Barrow III.

For my parents

MARTHA E. HURD
1917–2005

DONALDSON B. HURD
1917–2002

Every time we walk along a beach some ancient urge
disturbs us so that we find ourselves shedding shoes
and garments or scavenging among seaweed and
whitened timbers like the homesick refugees of a long war.

— LOREN EISELEY

from black-flowering to light-flowering we name them,
from barest conception, the almost not thought of, to heaviest
matter, we name them,
from glacier-lit blue to the gold of iguana we name them,
and naming, begin to see,
and seeing, begin to assemble the plain stones of earth.

— JANE HIRSHFIELD

Contents

Acknowledgments

Some of these essays, in one version or another, first appeared in other publications.

"Wordwrack: Openings" was originally published in *Brevity* (Summer 2007).

"Moon Snail" was originally published in *Short Takes*, ed. Judith Kitchen (New York: W. W. Norton, 2005).

"Wentletrap" originally appeared in *Orion*.

"Pebbles" was originally published as "Fine Distinctions" in *Fourth Genre*, published by the Michigan State University Press. It also appeared in *The Pushcart Prize* (New York: W. W. Norton, 2008).

"Purple Sailors" originally appeared in the *Los Angeles Times*.

"Bits of Clay, Glass, Wood," revised from the originally titled piece "Finding and Making," was first published by Haystack.

A huge thanks to my agent, Cynthia Cannell, for her wise guidance, to my husband, Stephen Dunn, for his clear eye and unwavering support, to Frostburg State University for a sabbatical during which I finished the manuscript, and to the Thursday night writing group for invaluable suggestions and vital camaraderie.

Walking the Wrack Line

1 BROKEN OAR
Preface

Let us look for secret things
somewhere in the world
on the blue shore of silence.
— PABLO NERUDA

I WAS IN MY MIDFORTIES before I understood that you don't always have to see where you're going in order to get there. Whoever insists otherwise prizes purposeful action over the accidents of vision. Sometimes they're right, though I never saw ahead of me so many worthwhile places where I've ended up: that former lobster shack, for example, where I lived alone one summer near a boutique-filled town north of Boston. I'd gone there with two dogs and big plans to write a biography of Celia Thaxter, the nineteenth-century writer who'd grown up on an island nine miles off the nearby New Hampshire coast. Standing on the beach one day, squinting north, I imagined the Isle of Shoals, where Thaxter had lived, and tried to separate her reasons for staying in such a place from my own similar fantasies. What did she want out there in the endlessness of ocean and sky, in the day-after-day of blue-gray in every direction and nothing on any horizon? Perhaps the island was her watery version of wilderness, where she might, like Christ or a monk, expand her sense of the spiritual. That was an aspiration I, seldom sure where to look, understood.

Underfoot that day was the usual medley of seaweed and shells, bits of plastic and driftwood, the ordinary ravel of wrack line every high tide leaves behind. Though it seemed unlikely that any-thing spiritual might expand there on the beach — dogs yanking on their leashes, lobster pots piled precariously high, boats up on cradles for repair, and everywhere the smell of fish — it felt good to be moving, to stop now and then and watch the small dot of a freighter way offshore, headed down the Atlantic coast. A few yards from me, a man fussed with a camera, and just down-rock from their parents, four or five children watched the boats and gulls and tossed stones into the water. Several walked along the edge, bending over to pick up bits of beach debris.

Out in the harbor to my left, a dozen small sailboats practiced their maneuvers, tacking port then starboard in choreographed glissades of clean white triangles. Like sailors everywhere, they must have studied the jetty and shoals ahead and laid out a course to avoid them. Behind me, the narrow streets were crowded with sunglassed people who wove between slow-moving cars and chil-dren with ice cream cones. Wandering on the beach, I watched an object out in the waves, spent twenty minutes trying to figure out what it was. It hadn't bobbed so much as ridden, appearing on the top of a wave, disappearing behind it. Its rhythmic lift and sink had made it hard to identify — large fish? a log? a swimmer's rubber flipper? The closer it got, the flatter it looked, floating like some-thing wooden, and by the time the skim of water twirled it clock-wise and left it in the jumble of wrack, I could see it was a plank of some sort, a crafted thing, not a limb or something drowned, and then, finally, that it was a broken oar.

∾

I was twelve when my parents returned from the Bahamas with a lie they must have thought would comfort me and with a basket of shells I understood as a bribe. Somehow I knew they'd gone for that week in an effort to save their marriage. They came back with careful smiles and gave me the basket as an offering — or was it a bargain? *Take these*, they seemed to say — tiger shells and fluted conchs. *Look at these, instead of at us.*

The shells, all highly polished and in perfect condition, were clearly purchased at some souvenir stand, not scavenged from the beach. That made me even lonelier. I remember positioning the shells on my bureau with their openings facing each other, pretending their apertures were mouths so some conversation might ensue. Later, turning the back of one to the other or moving them to opposite corners, I created visible dramas for the invisible ones I must have known were taking place behind closed doors. Maybe for a while that sufficed.

I don't credit my parents with the longings that deepened over the years. If they induced these feelings at all, it was through the gift of the failure of their gift, the possibility that those exquisite shells on my dresser helped me to see the difference between the lie of the perfectly preserved versus the venture of the salvaged and transformable. I'm more interested these days in what might be rescued — from near destruction, from invisibility, from silence.

໖

On the morning I found the oar, however, nothing mattered but a break from work. Finding it didn't solve the problem of the biography or the crowded shack or the dogs' short tempers. I couldn't even tell what might have happened to whoever once held the oar, if the person had rowed blindly backward into something that crunched the bow and wrenched the oars, splintered them into the surf. In a rowboat without an oar, you're at the mercy of current and wave, helpless to control the direction or stability of your craft. Maybe the guy drowned; maybe he made it to shore, or maybe he was miles away when the oar somehow got pitched into the sea. All that remained was gray and smooth, the length of an arm, consisting of a blade and six inches of shaft. The round section that human hands might have clenched was nowhere in sight.

But finding it did remind me how good it can feel to walk aimlessly at the edge of the ocean. I found a bone the next day, and then a strand of horsetail kelp, a bit of driftwood that looked exactly like the letter K. Later, a spider crab, whose young, I learned, often hitchhike inside a jellyfish's bell. Each time: an object first and sometimes a place for it in the shack. None of them added up to clear reasons for Thaxter's choice to live out there in such remote and sea-swept isolation.

My book that lobster-shack summer was *Moby-Dick*, its magnificent whale and the sense of imminence: something was always out there, not too far ahead. If you're the hero, your job is to pursue it. I envied the surety of Ahab's quest, no matter how ill-conceived. How remarkable, I thought then, to be driven by such a clear mission. I wanted for myself a belief that could keep me similarly fixed on a single course, some kind of guide that could dictate every difficult decision. I spent many a morning during those hot months, pacing on the shore, watching the horizon, listening to the foghorn, thinking about Melville's image of the sea as "the ungraspable phantom of life." I knew my mother would understand that image, though she feared the water, wasn't much of a reader, and never spoke of the hungers I was sure she must have. And I knew my father would not, though he was a sailor who studied navigational charts as diligently as he did the newspaper. Reading that Melville line, she might do a painting, mix her oils to approximate the color of longing; he might dismiss her, wrinkle his brow, worry about shifting shoals that could ground a boat. Perhaps such marked contrasts help explain a child who learned to do what many children of estranged parents do, which is to navigate the vacancies between them. Or to stay, as I often did, almost out of reach in an oddly rich remoteness, missing what I didn't know I didn't have.

ᕬ

I still love the sound of oarlocks, those bronze, U-shaped devices mounted on the gunwales to hold an oar in place and act as a fulcrum for rowing — their creak and clang as they simultaneously swivel and hold while the oars dip in again and again. Unlike every other means of locomotion — cars, horses, bicycles — rowing a boat requires that you turn your back to where you're going. To move forward in a rowboat you face the stern, bend over the oars, and pull, lifting your head to watch not what's ahead, but what you're leaving behind: the dock stinking of diesel fuel and fish, or home. Each ply of the oars makes that world grow smaller, and meanwhile you keep your back to the bow while some destination approaches from behind.

The Awful Rowing toward God, claimed the poet Anne Sexton, who had looked so many things — death, sex, despair — square in the face. Attach an image to that title: the rounded bent-over-the-oars spine and the eyeless back of the skull leading the way toward what she imagined was divine. Awful, she must have thought, to have to draw near that way, unable to see what you're moving toward. There's a long history, though, of being told to avert one's eyes; when the Lord ensconced Moses in a stone cleft on Mt. Sinai, he said, "You shall see my back; but my face shall not be seen." In churches and mosques and temples all over the world, we bow our heads, we close our eyes, we lie face down on the floor, we know the admonishments against peeking.

Or maybe Sexton's rowing doesn't have anything at all to do with not looking at something supposedly too glorious for our eyes. Maybe it has to do with keeping our sight on what's smack in front of us: our own hands, dirty or clean, the inescapable evidence of how we've lived our lives. *Let us pray*, some preacher says, and there before me are not only my fingernails chewed to the quick, but also my feet caked with the evidence of where I've been — sand or mud or leaf litter clinging to the soles — all my anxieties and impatience and wandering habits that I ought, I suppose, to be praying about.

I took the oar that day on the Rockport beach and shoved the broken shaft down into sand. It stood there, blade up, like a traffic cop's hand as if to signal wait, stop, no more making this more than it is: a broken oar, sea-scarred and useless. Right, I reminded myself, chagrined again by my urge to mythologize so much of what I see. The rower's position in the boat has only to do with the strength of back muscles, the relative power of push versus pull, not with some poet's angst about God or our own about the past.

Out in the harbor, the sailboats tacked again to starboard and the man with the camera left without taking a single shot of the oar I'd stuck in the sand. And why should he? Why would anyone take the time for a broken oar? But evidently many do; there's a Broken Oar Bar on an Illinois river, and in Moab, Utah, a Broken Oar Restaurant. On the Maryland coast, a Broken Oar Grill; a Broken Oar Pub in North Dakota. On their rooftops and menus, in their lobbies and ads: broken oars outlined in neon or sketched in ink, the splintered shafts reminders of ruin, and inside, a cozy bar, sometimes a fireplace, the warmth of camaraderie, a safe harbor to return to. There must be some appeal to a broken oar, its weathered look and imperfections, the tired way it welcomes: if your means of navigation has failed, left you drifting or beached, you might as well swim or wade or hitch a ride to the dock, come in, pull up a stool and sit a spell, tell us all what happened.

I abandoned the Thaxter biography a week after I found the oar. I didn't know how to salvage its few good moments, any more than I knew what might have saved my parents' or my own first marriage. Plans fail, friendships fall apart; what was precious to me in my twenties seemed banal in my thirties. In my forties, I realized that a lot of what I care about in the world survives in spite of — perhaps because of — having been lost for a while in the backward drift of childhood or middle-age morass. Now in my fifties, I may be simply wishing to chart the evolution of curiosity and the clearing-out that accompanies my own aging. Or perhaps, more elusively, to understand the ways my parents and the silence of our house seemed to empty the world and therefore, ironically, to open it.

The details don't matter — they belong to all of us — and loss, after all, is mostly a story about what happens next. What's next for me, it seems, is the story of realizing that if there are answers at all, they might not be found in the broadest expanses. I find myself mostly lowering my habitual gaze-out-to-sea and settling down to rummage in these greenish-brown, often stinking, bug-infested wrack lines, the likes of which I must have skirted or stepped over thousands of times in my younger-me rush to get to the water. Sometimes I notice what lies tangled within them: the moon snail with its grotesque foot, trash turned into sea glass, driftwood, egg cases, jellyfish. And sometimes I notice what's gone. Not just my grandiose quest, but also the vanished tangible.

On the beach that next day, the oar, for example, had disappeared. I'll never know if it got wedged in the jetty just west of the cove or displayed in a craft shop, festooned with gauzy mermaids or ceramic anchors. Am I looking for clues? I'd like to think not. The wrack line, after all, is not some hieroglyphic the gods leave twice a day for us to decipher. Yet it's hard to resist; we're doomed, it seems, to try to make meaning. And if, as Neruda says, "faint signs are left," the least we can do is try to figure out how to look at what's here — all these small things that the sea, arriving like an empty-handed guest, nevertheless keeps handing out as gifts. I don't know yet how, if at all, these objects are connected, what kind of coherence they might suggest. But they are what I wish to study now — their physicality, their form and weight, the way they live or lie ruined or changed right in front of me.

2 WORDWRACK

Openings

> Jewelry, tides, language:
> things that shine.
> What is description, after all,
> but encoded desire?
> — MARK DOTY

A NOR'EASTER SMACKED INTO CAPE ANN last night, and this morning the wrack's dark line lies tangled and heaped. Hundreds of shells have settled sideways and tilted on the beach, half in, half out, sand-dribbled, seaweed-draped, partially rinsed. On the outside, they're a riot of spires and pinpricks, ribbed turbans and knobby cones. Ivory, copper, pinkish, twisted, scalloped, hinged.

In the cool and sunny aftermath of the storm, I squat down, close my eyes, scoop them up, and let them cascade through my fingers. Nothing whole seems to make it to the beach, the ocean itself being the great agent of breakage. So much of what washes ashore here has been pummeled by waves, dragged on gritty bottoms. The pressure of sea overhead can cause fragile clams to shatter, unhinge, and crack open. Something about this enlivens me.

Inside, the shells are emptied or crammed full of the creatures that created them: waved whelk and wentletraps, oysters and scallops, some of them dead, others trying to get back into the water or dry out a bit in the sand. Their narratives do nothing to distinguish them. Eat, protect, reproduce, and die: what else is new? This, the language of how they do it: scuttle and siphon, burrow and spit, scissor-step and sink.

When I open my eyes, the ocean seems to demand too much. At another time in my life, I might have responded — raised a sail, plied my oars, at least considered the lure of infinity. If the sea, after all, has any constant call that can also sound like taunting, it goes like this: *come in, come in.* But this is the cold north Atlantic and I'm older and I won't and besides, if I did, I'd be out there immersed in the lives of these cracked-open things I'd rather look at underfoot. It's not that I'm tired of desire; I just want to make sure it's my own.

Wherever the sea — like others' wants — begins to encroach, there's evidence of scrimmage. Here, crab claws and feathers, fraying rope and shredded kelp, an upended dory and a man I avoid because he wants to talk again about shamanic journeys. I'm less interested at the moment in where things are going, more in what happens if they come apart.

Without its creature of needs, an emptied shell allows me to see the curve of a marblelike entrance, to note that light diminishes as it travels up the coil. I can even stick a finger in. Close to my left foot lies the upper valve of a jingle shell; the underside of its shallow dome gleams silvery yellow and translucent, a scraping of mica. Here on the boundary between broken and whole, insides glisten, and my current favorite, a blue mussel edged in violet, lies opened against a cockleshell whose interior is the color of yolk.

3 MOON SNAIL
Unseemly Proportions

No very small animal can be beautiful, for
looking at it takes so small a portion of time
that the impression of it will be confused.
— ARISTOTLE

SURELY ARISTOTLE'S WRONG. If a moon snail isn't beautiful, it's not because it's small. This shell I've just lifted out of sand, in fact, is a graceful whorl of bluish grays that pale toward white. When I turn it to the sun, the luster of plum glazing the aperture shines almost luminescent. It's been at sea for a while, no trace of the creature inside. I run my pinky finger up into the emptied chamber. If I were a painter like my mother, I'd paint this with other objects whose interiors beckon: geodes, kiwis, bells. Forgoing the richness of Dutch masters — a polished table, a pitcher, and always that yellow light pouring through a window — I'd set my easel up on the beach, frame my objects with pieces of driftwood, position them in a tangle of seaweed. Drawn as I am to the evidence of departure, my painting would include prints in the sand — crab claws, human feet, dog paws, the wide and meandering band the moon snail leaves behind. Beauty, it seems to me, must have something to do with movement both inward and away.

Moon snails are carnivores. They kill with their feet and their tongues. Sensing a nearby clam just under the surface of sand, a moon snail pumps water in rippling waves to its own retracted foot, which soon emerges as a swelling gelatinous nub that grows into one of the largest of all snail feet, four times the size of its own shell. A shapeless, boneless appendage smeared with mucous, it keeps pulsing, spreading forward and sideways until the shell itself sits slightly lifted, almost encircled, and the pulpy thing with its whorled carriage oozes forward. The propodium — the front edge of the foot — plows the sand aside, much like a cowcatcher on the front end of a train.

I try to imagine the buried clam, wonder whether it can feel the unstable sand above, the sense of something large approaching, about to make a tomb. And then the foot shoveling down, settling on, wrapping around, like a live and fleshy blanket.

A clam is a bivalve; it can shut its shell, stay closeted until danger has passed. There's plenty of room inside, and no way for a moon snail to pry anything open. The foot tightens around the clam. Perhaps for a moment there's great stillness.

And then the moon snail's tongue — coiled, studded with small rounded teeth, rasplike — begins to lick a small hole in the clam's shell. It licks and licks and once in a while it releases a little juice. The juice corrodes. The giant foot clenches the clam. The tongue grazes and scrapes and finally breaks through, making a neatly beveled hole.

Just below, trapped inside its hinged shell, the clam must feel a sudden trickle of sand, a poof of air. And then the prod of a long proboscis.

What does it look like, that initial suck? Does tissue bubble, a dimple rising into the proboscis? A dimple that spreads and deepens until the body is nothing else, just this rising and rising like a small spout of gray tissue drawn up into the straw, the mouth, into the body of the moon snail, which looms above it?

Perhaps my painting must be a diptych. In the second panel, the aftermath: emptied clamshells with neatly bored holes near their hinges.

And maybe the moon snail itself, when hunger's been replaced by danger and it needs to gather up that large and fleshy foot and disappear inside itself. An approaching sea star can trigger its retreat, as can the nearing plow of another snail or a gull's growing shadow. The foot starts to contract its muscle, expel water from its flesh. It grows dry and begins to recede inside its own shell, which looks now much too small to hold it. When the last protruding nub has been pulled inside, the operculum, a hornlike oval door, closes, seals the snail inside and out of reach.

It can't breathe for long with such a thing inside. Its gills are pressed against its heart and stomach, smushed against the inside wall. It must feel claustrophobic, crowded by the very thing it needs to stay alive.

Once the moon snail has shown its foot, it cannot be called beautiful. Aristotle notwithstanding, this has nothing to do with size but with unseemly proportions and the reminder that need so often vulgarizes form. My painting, I see now, should be a triptych. I'd want the last panel to suggest that a certain beauty recedes when hunger and threats intensify. There'd be sand dunes in the distance and a horde of snails in the foreground, their insides grotesque and efficient, on the verge of suffocating themselves.

4 EGG

Breaking Out

SOMEWHERE ON THIS ISLAND OF ST. CROIX a chick has managed to break out of its egg or a mongoose has lain down with full belly. What the shell in my hand might say about the difference between confinement and protection can't matter to either one. To me, though, it's a tangible reminder of the delicate line — physical and psychological — that can separate one creature's birth from another's appetite.

The sand beneath my bare feet is fine and white; the turquoise sea surrounds. Except for its jagged edge, the fragment of egg in my hand is flawlessly curved, its chalky whiteness mottled only by nest stains. If I use this ladle-sized shard to imagine the rest, I'd guess it would have been twice as big as a chicken egg. A man walking by, binoculars in hand, says it's a brown pelican egg. They're endangered, he reminds me, threatened by nest-raiding mongooses all over the island.

A pelican looks like a cross between heron and turkey, a primitive silhouette in the sky made comic by the jowly throat pouch that dangles below. But there's nothing primitive about its eggs, which, like all eggs, suggest artistic triumph — an absolutely smooth curve even the best potters struggle to achieve. No seams or bulge, nothing off center, not a single skewed plane and no sign of beginning or end, not even a hint of how to get out or in. Even more remarkable is the soundness of their structure. Take an egg, lay it in your palm, and try to crush it with your fingers. It'll sit in your hand like a stone.

Imagine, then, the mongoose's dilemma. He's found a nest with a couple of eggs, endured the parents' close swoops, their squawking alarms. The egg's between his paws, but the shell's too strong to shatter. He has to roll it away from the nest, position it near some object — a rock, a wall, a tree — lie down on his side, and hurl it against the hard surface.

The seawater is warm. When I slosh a little into the shell piece, the edges crumple a bit; a few cracks form. Like so many things, it's much more fragile when it isn't whole. I dry it with the hem of my T-shirt and try to picture the long-beaked, unborn chick nestled against the inside curve, the first — perhaps the only — horizon it would have known. There's no seeing through the thin layer of calcite, though if I hold it up to my eye and pass my other hand between the shell and the sun, I can make a shadow and then make it darker. To be inside must seem like being inside a perfectly round tent of starched white sheets on the night of a full moon. If it could have opened its eyes, would the chick have seen its approaching mother as a shadow looming closer? Could it have distinguished between her and the pointy snout of a predator? On the beach, there's no sign of the nest or the rest of the shell, which ought to be nearby, and no sign of the bird. No way to tell whether the chick freed itself or felt its egg crack in two against a tree.

Mechanical engineers have determined it's easier to break out of an egg than to break into one. The reason has to do with the shape of a shell's crystals. Near my home in western Maryland, there's an old, single-span stone arch bridge at whose engineering I've often marveled. How has it stayed there for almost two hundred years, enduring horses, carriages, and then cars? The principle of any arch is this: The stones are wedge-shaped, the narrower ends pointed down, toward the inside of the arch, so that if you exert pressure on the top, you're only compressing the spaces between stones, making the structure sturdier. But if you get underneath and bang up with a sledgehammer, the stones will slide up and out of their interlocked positions, and the arch will collapse on top of you. The calcite shells of an egg are similarly shaped, so the mongoose pawing at a pelican egg is often stymied, but the damp, folded-over chick pecking away from the inside is not.

Getting out, however, isn't as easy as opening a door. The thing within still has to work for its own freedom. The pelican chick grows with its curved neck pressed against an air bubble lodged in the large end of the egg. When four weeks have passed, rising levels of carbon dioxide inside the egg trigger the muscles on the back of its neck to spasm and thus the egg tooth on the top of the beak bangs against the bubble, which finally breaks open. The chick gets its first gulp of oxygen and rests. Then it begins to peck against the shell itself. It pecks and pecks. Because its right wing keeps its head locked in one position, every whack with the egg tooth hits the shell at about the same place and avoids the mis-hits I make with hammer and nail. No matter how precise I try to be, my walls are dimpled with haphazard marks all around the intended target. But the chick wields its egg tooth like an accurate pickaxe; it jabs and pokes in a single small circle until it's chipped a hole big enough to wiggle through. Houdini without hidden tools, the chick takes hours to free itself. A whooping crane takes two days. An albatross takes up to six. Imagine the exhaustion, the shambles of birth.

In my library at home I once counted four books with photos of unbroken eggs on their covers. Two are art books, one's a book about journeys, and one of them — a philosophical text titled *Six Names of Beauty* — features Brancusi's elegantly curved marble egg called *Sculpture for the Blind*. It's a luminous reminder of Samuel Butler's comment that a bird "is only an egg's way of making another egg." Ironic, how exquisitely complete an egg looks, as if it were the final product and not the about-to-be-torn-apart start. Beauty aside, an egg's going to break or rot from the inside out, or it's going to be broken into. It's that inevitability I'm also reminded of here on a beach — the shattering you can't undo or pretend hasn't happened.

Birth, in fact, is one of the few big events in any creature's life that do not allow for ambivalence. Countless opportunities later for hesitation and reversals, backtracking and never-minds, for staying halfway in and halfway out of whatever seems to bind. But not at the beginning. Once the first crack has been made, there's no going back, no opting to delay for a few more days. Some ancient process is set in motion and there's nothing to do but ride it out.

Fortunately or unfortunately, in the realm of human psychology, one birth is probably never enough. At every stage of development there might be another shell to emerge from — parental protection, constraining relationships, antiquated ideas of home, one's own outdated image of self. How many times, I've sometimes wondered, can one keep doing this? How many redefinitions?

To try to escape from what confines is an instinct, evidently programmed for life. Ornithologists used to believe otherwise: that hatching behavior was short-lived, triggered inside the shell and then diminishing after birth. But recent research indicates that if you take any bird of any age — a young warbler, male or female, a middle-aged swallow, an old screech owl — and tuck its head under the right wing just so, it'll begin again to try to break out. The moves are the same and oddly recognizable: It rotates its shoulders, thrusts its legs in a kind of get-me-out-of-here frenzy. It hammers the air with its beak. There's no egg in sight, no shell obscuring its vision, no visible wall it's fighting through. How familiar and poignant all this is: the muscle-buried memory of the need to emerge, to lift one's head from under one's own wing.

I don't know what happened to the bird whose egg pieces I crumple in my hand. It broke out or the predator broke in. If I'd been present when the mongoose approached the nest, what would I have done? How long might I have stood, weighing the beauty of the egg with its suggestion of fruition against the cunning of the mongoose obeying his own hungers? If the man with the binoculars had come up the beach at just the right moment, I imagine he would have found a stick and done what he felt compelled to do. I would have envied his decisiveness.

5 SPIDER CRAB
Disguise

Camouflage is a game we all like to play, but our
secrets are as surely revealed by what we want to
seem to be as by what we want to conceal.

— RUSSELL LYNES

FOR YEARS, I HOARDED FIELD GUIDES on everything from
birds' eggs to fossils. They cluttered my desk and dining room
table, bathroom counter and mudroom bench. I still love them
for the precision with which they describe eyestalks and hinges,
and for the promise they make: you can pick up almost anything
anywhere and track down its family, genus, and species by measur-
ing size, counting bumps, distinguishing, say, between purple and
indigo stains. You can name it, and I like that reward for paying
attention.

But lately, I've been more aware that field guides can also per-
petuate the delusion that once you've named a thing you know
what it is. Take the shell a child showed me earlier this morning.
She'd kicked it up out of the sand, she said. Did I know what it
was? Yellow-tan, triangular, covered with what felt like calcified
pimples, no remnant of creature inside, no trace of muscle or flesh.
Down the middle of its back ran a line of bumps. *It feels like plastic,* I told her. Its shell seemed so fragile I wondered aloud how it
had protected whatever used to live inside. Though I could make
a good guess, I turned to the girl, who seemed to be waiting, and
asked what she thought.

Clam? she suggested.

I shook my head. *Clams would have some evidence of a hinge.*

I pulled a field guide from my pocket and turned to the illustrations of crabs.

Comparing object to drawings, we could see it didn't belong to a mole crab (too small), or a purse crab (too rounded), or a porcelain (too spotted). Then, a matching image and this description: "shell strongly tubercled; about 9 spines along center of back. Brown to dull yellowish." There was no mistaking; it was the shell of a spider crab. *Spider crab*, she repeated. And then she thanked me, put the shell in her pocket, and disappeared down the beach.

I knew immediately I'd failed her. She had the name now and that pleased her. I imagined her pulling the shell out of her pocket later and showing her friends, perhaps a sibling or parents. *See?* she might say, *It's a spider crab.* Maybe they'll turn it over, run their fingers over the spine, but chances are by tomorrow they'll have forgotten the name. Or if they haven't, they'll do what most of us might: think of cobwebs and claws, a dark, scrabbly thing they wouldn't want crawling up their necks. The name does, in fact, come from its appearance — round body held up by long legs. And it's true that the largest of them have bodies fifteen inches across; their legs, all ten of them, span fifteen feet — the width of a typical American bedroom. That kind lives in deep ocean-floor vents off the coast of Japan and would make good monsters for horror films.

But here on the Atlantic coast they're just a few inches wide, and, like all spider crabs — those giant ones near Japan included — they're a lot of show and not a lick of danger. The truth is a spider crab is sluggish and innocuous. Its waving pincers are mostly bluff, incapable of killing. It eats dead things. Whether the girl with her shell will ever know that — or anything else about how spider crabs survive — I don't know. What was it I didn't give her?

❧

I first learned about a spider crab's habit of masquerade when, as a junior in high school, I wrote a term paper hypothesizing that All Saints' Day actually evolved from the mischief and masquerade of the night before and not vice versa. In other words, I claimed Halloween was not a recently sanctioned night of pent-up revelry before a long-established holy day, but that the holy day evolved as a way of absolving the pointless mania of the night before. Nothing dissuaded me, neither the absence of a shred of supporting evidence nor an F on the paper. I was in my purist mode then, disdainful of excess and sure of the need to chasten through prayer. Not much remains of that piety, but that research on masquerade back then led me to the spider crab.

When it isn't scavenging, the spider crab is usually absorbed by costumes. I mean this literally. It spends its time bedecking itself in underwater finery. Because it's slow and defenseless and its shell is thin, the crab's primary means of protection is to go unnoticed, to blend in with its surroundings. It begins by drooling spit onto its front claws and coating its shell with the mucousy adhesive. Then, with a sluggish lurch, the spider crab lifts its spiny carapace aloft on ten legs and sets off in its underwater world to collect camouflage. It isn't picky. It plucks a tuft of bright blue sponge with its pincers and fastens it to its back, glues a morsel of sea lettuce near its head. If the mucous isn't adhesive enough, it uses the short, barbed hairs that stud its body. Extending a claw to nearby kelp, it snares a strand, hitches it under the hook. The kelp trails like a veil.

❧

The Halloween I was fourteen and full of contempt for costume parties and makeup, my mother took me shopping for a winter coat and kept pulling green ones off the racks — pea coats in emerald and apple green, a dressy coat in moss, even a cape in something almost lime. *Green's a good color for you,* she said. *Nice with your hair and skin tones.*

Too bright, I countered. *Maybe something brown?*

She picked a jade one off a rack, led me to a mirror, and held it up to my shoulders. *See?* she asked.

In the mirror was a girl I hardly knew. Splashy. Loud. Vivid. Did I know Toulouse-Lautrec's paintings back then? I looked like one of his subjects, one he'd painted a dozen times. Is that how my own mother wanted me to be? Behind me, Paris and a whole history of gallery shows, thousands of people walking by, examining this or that detail of my portrait. And then my mother's face beside mine in the mirror, her hands still pressing the jade shoulders into mine, the price tag dangling from a sleeve.

See? Can you see what it does to your hair? Turns it golden. And your face? More vibrant. Now look. She whisked the coat away and held a camel one under my chin. *Blur your eyes,* she suggested, and I watched myself become a blend of browns: light brown hair, tanned skin, brown eyes, tan coat.

Ugh, she whispered, *you look like a sand dune.*

How to tell her I loved that comparison? All those shadings, the shadows on its curves, the way something as invisible as wind could change its shape.

Like your paintings? I tried reminding her. She knew I loved them.

You're not a painting. You're a person.

For her, clothes had something to do with vivacity, with how certain colors complement each other and might make a person seem more alive. I thought back then they had more to do with shelter, how, for instance, tan can darken into terra umbra and save a person from others' superficial scrutiny.

She couldn't stand the sand dune coat and I couldn't bear the jade. I tried on gray ones, she brought me blue. I thought of the argument then as one of style over substance, display over sound character. The loneliness between us was like that, I think now: good intentions to connect, some feeble attempts, sensibilities that only mystified. We went home with nothing new.

It took a midlife crisis years later to help me see that my mother was partly right about choices to dress up, and that field guides help with spider crabs only after they're dead and washed up with their nine spines undisguised. That was the year I devoured books like Sheehy's *Passages* and some therapist's *So You Too Want to Be an Artist?* and hated them all. They nailed me on too many pages, made my secret habits and quirky defenses sound like those of every other woman re-examining her life. I couldn't stand being so easily recognizable. I wanted my griefs to be completely mine, the consolation friends offered tailored to my own brand of angst. Not that matching of emotion to chapter, of solace to an index of remedies. In crisis, it seems, we're often much alike, reduced to a dozen predictable responses, pretty easily identifiable and therefore less our own quirky selves. Which is good for labeling crab shells but not so good for the individuality most of us humans want to believe in.

No wonder our tendency to masquerade.

∾

If I didn't know better, I'd say the spider crab must have a sense of play — foppish, festooned, good-humored in its finery. It even allows others to burrow in and make a home in the midst of its masquerade. Hitchhikers and long-term tenants — small colonies of jellyfish and barnacles — fasten themselves to the algae that's fastened to the crab and, like residents of a multistory apartment complex, go lurching along the ocean floor.

The generosity reminds me of a man I once knew, and in his case, too, generosity masked a fierce self-protection. He gave money to charities, money to friends, money to small artists' communes in the deserts of India. But unlike the spider crab, what he wanted was to have his generosity recognized so that he could continue to hide. He paraded his gifts to protect his privacy, keep a certain distance.

Drop this display, I said to him once. *Show me your real self. Be with me naked.* And when he was, he looked pretty much like every other naked man I've seen. Four limbs, ears on the sides of the head, two forward-facing eyes, and genitals like any other. Stripped, ironically *un*revealed, no closer to intimacy at all.

❧

A spider crab can survive, if need be, by eating its own mask. If food is scarce, it will twist its front pincers around to its own back, pluck a morsel of algae growing there, and eat it. Mask ingestion, they call it. But at what point does ingestion matter more than protection? If each time a creature dines out on its own masquerade and leaves a little more of itself exposed, how far will it go? When it comes to crabs, the answer is clear: a crab will eat up to 4 percent of its own camouflage every day. If just a few mussels are around, it will limit itself to less than 3 percent. That's all. For the crab, evidently, protection trumps nourishment; it'd rather starve than expose itself.

For humans, I don't know. Perhaps for us, too, being naked — that is, exposed as ordinary — is scarier than being undernourished. Up to a certain point, we keep our costumes on, though that could mean a little hunger. We might even maintain the façade while underneath some part of us is starving.

The crab of course can't consider the dilemma this way. It does what it does out of instinct. Dressed up like a slow-moving, algae-festooned stone, it fools gulls and observers like me and can live for several years. Alive, no two ever look alike and the field guides I still treasure are useless. Undressed, they're identically dead and I can key one out in six seconds flat.

"Nature loves to hide," claimed Heraclitus. But for humans this hiding, I see now, is about more than just not wanting to be found; it's about not wanting to be reduced, not wanting our lives to fit tidily into some page in *Field Guide to the Human Mammal* — dates, places, life span, and eating habits. We want our lives to be idiosyncratically ours. And so we dress up — in clothing, attitudes, postures — and, ironically, reveal more surely who we are far better than we do when we're unadorned. Masquerade, after all, reveals how it is we wish to be disguised, what parts of us we want in the foreground, what parts in the background. It doesn't camouflage so much as announce our secret wishes.

I missed a chance with the girl on the beach. I should have kept the field guide in my pocket. I should have asked her how a crab with such a thin shell could survive, why it might be covered with little spines. I should have encouraged her questions, helped her connect observable details to stories of survival. Then I could have told her about the spider crab's need to masquerade. She might have understood something more about disguise, perhaps even begun to think about her own ploys and presentations, the ways she — like most of us — might deny hungers in order to feel safe.

As for me, I see now that even my old preference for shades of brown over bright jade greens had to do — much as I resisted this — with masquerade. I still love those colors and the task of distinguishing among them — khaki, fawn, cocoa, burnt almond. And among the meanings of shade: hue, tinge, trace, hint. But I realize now that what I wanted wasn't so much to hide in monotony but to signify my fondness — need? — for subtleties and shadows. I secretly wanted to be known — perhaps still do — as someone who prefers margins over the limelight.

I could, I suppose, follow the girl's tracks in the sand and, if I find her, give her another shell to identify. I'll keep the field guide in my pocket and show her only what might lead her to make finer distinctions — scalloped or toothed, flat-clawed or broad? If she grows impatient and asks for the book, I'll remind her that merely naming a thing doesn't mean you know what it is.

Preachy? Presumptuous? I suppose so. And not likely to occur. If the stories and disguises we adopt reveal more about who we are than any nakedness can, then I'll admit: I'm the kind of person who'd choose a Thomas Merton costume over a Tammy Faye. I'd find irresistible all those shadowy folds in simple woolen robes, the garden retreat, and the silence he pledged. I'd likely leave that girl alone.

6 STONES
Turning Points

Who placed us with eyes between a
microscopic and a telescopic world?
— THOREAU

THE SHORE WAS MY MOTHER'S FAVORITE SUBJECT, but in the
foreground of her paintings I can't recall a single object — never a
boat or bird, not even a rock or shell. If my mother were here on
the Maine coast with me this afternoon, easel in the sand, she'd be
painting the wild skies and disheveled ocean, but there'd be no broken oar in the foreground of her canvas, no daughter rearranging
stones on the beach. Even the grasses would seem less like singular
blades, more like elongated blurs — inconsequential, a means of
getting to what preoccupied her more: what was above or behind,
even beyond.

In one of her paintings, the sea seems to be rising into the sky,
an uplift of metal, lit up from within, reaching into the clouds'
swirling grains. I used to wonder how she achieved that combus-
tion of platinum and silver and how old she was when she discovered which compelled her more: water and fog or the people
and things that traveled through them. Were there failed seascapes
somewhere in the attic, their foregrounds littered with spars and
brown kelp, the handle of a child's broken shovel, maybe even a
clam digger bent over his bucket? Or did she know from the start
it was distant possibilities that commanded her attention?

Without her on this mid-July late afternoon, surprisingly cool and storm-imminent, I pile rocks on top of rocks with the intention of watching them fall down. I haven't consulted a chart but know from the narrowing exposed mud that the tide is on its way in. I figure I have a couple of hours. Working without a plan, I stack and ring, balance and wedge, glancing now and then at the water, which eases toward me almost imperceptibly. The stones take on personalities — one so quirkily jagged and unstackable it needs to be its own monument. Another just right for a rampart; a few flat ones, perfectly shaped for a threshold. In the spaces between large, lined-up stones, I press pebbles into mud, like cobbles in an alley. On the tops of flat rocks, I steady smaller ones, and on top of those, even tinier ones. When I stand back to study what I've done, the array resembles a foot-high city of alleyways and towers, nothing my mother would ever have assembled.

∾

The Pueblos believed the sun wouldn't rise if they weren't there to watch it, and though I know better, it seems suddenly crucial to stay here and see the exact moment this tide turns. It should be easy; I know tidal charts are marked in minutes: high tide, say, at 11:43 or 4:16. Even without a watch, isn't that an observable moment? The water will approach and approach and then, as if there were some lever pulled, some click that reverses the direction, the water will halt, begin to recede. I'll know it will come up no further. I'll be able to mark the line of high water with a stick, do what I've never been able to do in my life — say, here, *this* is the turning point. Things — my routines, work, relationships, whatever seemed unsatisfying — would be different from then on. How many times have I made that pledge? Here at least there's a chance, and I can hype the symbolism for a little pleasure. A small pine branch from just up the bank serves well; I study high water marks on the shore, make a guess, and lay it parallel to the shoreline, fifteen feet inland from where the water now sloshes.

Meanwhile, in my hand: a chunk of granite the size of a chicken egg. Formed over three hundred million years ago from magma in the volcanic hotbed that ringed what's now Maine coast, it cooled below the surface for millions of years — cooled unevenly, spottily, certain minerals crystallizing first, others intruding later, speckling the molten rock with black mica, feldspar, and quartz. When the last glaciers retreated and the land rebounded, the overlying rock eroded until that granite, now hard and cold, lay exposed, susceptible to fracture or quarrying, worn by wind and water and more ice. And now, after thousands of years, this piece has tumbled to this beach where I can pick it up and place it on my palm.

I can still see the pink feldspar, shiny bits of mica and quartz, the concoction of some stone mason and a Fabergé egg designer with a pointillist bent, though there's nothing delicate about it. The granite from this part of Maine underlies Manhattan bridges and clads the Museum of Fine Arts in Boston. It holds up the New York County Courthouse and graces the JFK Memorial in Arlington National Cemetery. This stone, I decide, belongs on top of the largest one I've found so far. I try perching it there, like an oblong lookout, but can't decide which way it should lean: toward the cobbled land or the oncoming tide? Which requires more vigilance? My mother would have said the sea; I decide on the land.

I like the way stone feels so solid. And even though I know its history and probable future, I like, for now, the pleasure of lifting a single one. When I touch it, I can say, with a certain degree of confidence, *this is a stone*. I can run my fingers over its edges, lick its contours. I can't do that with water, my mother's element. I can see it, swim in it, cup a handful. But it's not possible to touch the sea. It's too amorphous, too vast, and, like too much thought of the formless spiritual, it finally numbs me, splatters my attention. At the edge of the ocean, it's the stones now that ground me. And because they make my back ache and my fingers raw, I'm learning which ones I can lift and which must remain where they are — a necessary lesson in limitations I hope will help me watch the stones — and perhaps my own too-precious ideas — collapse.

∾

"A thing of beauty is a joy forever," John Keats once said. I doubt that anyone who messes around with stones on the beach would agree with him. I'm thinking especially of that master tidal cairn builder Andy Goldsworthy, who arranges and balances big stones between tides. His work compels because, in many ways, it quarrels with Keats's long-revered notion of beauty's permanence. Goldsworthy isn't interested in forever and he isn't interested in joy. What he is interested in, however, is paradox, those yoked contradictions that sometimes hold elusive truths. In fact, the genius of Goldsworthy's work, for me, is his ability to make paradox so aesthetically pleasing.

Goldsworthy, of course, makes his art at the edge of the sea because he needs the incoming tide to undermine his cairns. But I'm also inclined to think that his work compels not just because of what the tide does but because the inevitable backdrop of the sea forces us to consider the cairn — which is discrete and well shaped — in juxtaposition with the sea, which is fluid and formless, behind it. The contrast is sharp: the amorphousness of the ocean emphasizes the concreteness of the cairn and vice versa.

And because the cairn is egg-shaped, it provides visual closure: our eye travels around its edges and arrives back at the beginning, perhaps imagines what's inside. The visual movement is one of convergence. If he were building here on the beach with me, I would be able to see his entire structure, could even circle it, examine it from all angles, have some confidence that there's nothing, visually at least, that's eluding me.

But he's not here, and what most of us know of his work is through photographs. In them, the sea stretches the eye sideways, up, and out toward the horizon. Its invitation is to distance, expansion, which reminds us how limited our vision is, how vast the sea and sky are, how impossible it is, as my mother might have said, to know even a fraction of them.

To see Goldsworthy's cairn at the tidal edge, then, is to have one's eye pulled simultaneously in and down in some satisfying visual closure *and* out and up in some unsettling, open-ended expansiveness. It isn't just the work itself, in other words, but the work in its carefully chosen setting that heightens the simultaneous experience of both form and formlessness, intimacy and distance.

My city needs an arena, I decide, a coliseum where opposing forces could battle it out. I'll try for arched doorways and tiered bleachers. Though it rarely happens, doesn't the conflict of certain ideas deserve dedicated spaces and audiences who know when to cheer? I roll a few big stones in a circle, ring the inside with smaller ones.

One of the most poignant paradoxes of Goldsworthy's sculptures is their relentless reminder that nothing lasts. That is their beauty, too, which, as Camus says, is unbearable because it offers us "for a minute the glimpse of an eternity." It's only a matter of time before the water softens the sand beneath the stones — his and mine —, rises over and destabilizes their bases, slides one stone and then another into the sea. I wonder if Goldsworthy knows Robert Frost's description of a poem as "a momentary stay against confusion." Perhaps he thinks of his outdoor work that way too — as structures on the sinking, sliding edge of the sea that for a moment constitute a figure, a form, *made* things that last a few hours, a reminder both of the great wash of the tides and our own mute and futile attempts to pause the inevitable.

But I think there's something else. If, as Goldsworthy says, "the beach is a great teacher," what is it we learn here? There's no news in the tide's return. If a tidal chart can tell us exactly when the agent of destruction will arrive and we build anyway, it doesn't seem like risk so much as a wish for timed transformation. We're in cahoots with the sea, not creating in defiance of its destruction.

Every tidal sculpture is doomed; Goldsworthy knows it and so do I. The making is done with an eye on the waves, which come up, sure enough, right on schedule. Constructing it there, it seems, must enact what we all do and don't want to know: that beauty built on the edge of the beach — maybe everywhere? — is in part beautiful because it cannot endure.

And look what guarantees its end: water — formless, transparent, one of the softest substances in the world. That's what will destroy the cairn and ultimately the stones themselves, which are nothing more than remnants of mountains we think of as stable, enduring. "Under heaven," the *Tao Te Ching* says, "nothing is more soft and yielding than water. / Yet for attacking the solid and strong, nothing is better; / It has no equal."

I toy with stones and memories and the lessons of paradox. Goldsworthy toys with ideas of stability and completion. He is, in fact, counting on a natural law: matter changes constantly, erodes, disintegrates, transforms into something else. If, as he reminds us, we live in a world where things are constantly evolving or devolving, metamorphosing, might that not be true of us too?

Watching the top rock on one of my towers topple, I think of another line by Keats: "'Beauty is truth, truth beauty,' — that is all / Ye know on earth, and all ye need to know." I doubt Goldsworthy would argue with that one. There's beauty in his work not only because it's aesthetically pleasing but also because it seems paradoxically true, meaning accurate, the way things are, how we really live our lives. We hover between form and formlessness. On some level we know nothing lasts, yet we cling to things as if they will. We pretend we don't need what we long for.

An hour later, the water begins to threaten my entire city. It inches quietly forward, no gush, no current I can see, just a small rising so gentle it doesn't seem to be coming from an oceanic tidal rhythm, but from an underwater spring inside this cove. The stones grow darker, wetter; they seem to stick their heads above the water. On the north side of the array, all the top rocks slip off their bases and disappear. But on the south they remain, better balanced, perhaps, or their bases more firmly pushed into mud. Gray granite, I see now, works better as a base than flint does. Pink granite has more ledges for pebbles. And mica-speckled granite is wasted on foundations — too soon covered by water. Sometimes when a thing collapses, I realize now, I have a chance to get to know it better.

∾

Years ago, my mother painted on the Jersey shore while my siblings and I built elaborate, moat-ringed castles with turrets and arched doorways. She loved the morning light gold-leafing the water; we loved the moment incoming tides spilled into our moat. She was thoughtful; we were happily frenzied, redirecting the water with plastic shovels and hastily dug channels, full of shrieks when the sea encircled. There was something graceful and noble about that destruction — the castle hand-patted into place and then softened into the sea — and about the way she'd turn and watch us then. What kept her from joining us? What, seeing us there, was she thinking? What we knew was the best sand was close to the water, that the tide would have its way, and we'd build regardless, as if part of the pleasure were seeing the ruin, which didn't feel aggressive, of course, but rhythmic: first you build it and then you tend its demolition. For us, fun. But as an adult, she would have felt the weight of such a rhythm. Was that what she couldn't — or wouldn't — find words to say?

∾

On the wall of our foyer is a photograph of a sand sculpture — a naked man and woman. The artist evidently began by digging a pit at the edge of the ocean. On its longer sloped side, he sculpted their two reclining bodies, feet down toward the center of the pit, torsos up the inclined edge. The woman is pressed up against the man's back. Her hand lies over his left shoulder. The rest of her body is invisible, behind his. From calves down, his legs are buried in sand. The work is finely wrought; it's easy to imagine touching the ribs, earlobes, toes, the folds of the cloth draped over his groin. I swear if I were there on that beach with them I could lift her finger.

The artist has fashioned their faces to make them look oblivious to the trough he's obviously dug to channel the sea across their heads and down around their torsos. Already the tide is coming in. They lie with their gaze upward, their backs slightly arched, the way one might in pleasure, submitting to the touch of another as the sea funnels under them. Or they look as if they've willingly crawled onto some sacrificial table, but instead of fire or knife, it's water that will do them in. Their bodies will dissolve, be taken back into the sea.

What did the artist want us to imagine they were feeling? Rapture? Some kind of sublime resignation? I think we, viewing it, are supposed to feel a sweet inexorability. Yes, my enigmatic mother might agree: Nobody can stop the tide from coming in, but the artist can heighten that exquisite pressure by building something beautiful just moments before it has to disappear.

◌

I watch the Maine tide for what seems like hours. The water rises and rises and every time I think it's halted, is about to recede, it slides up another inch, drowns another tower. Again and again, I have to move my pine branch inland, sure each time that the water will advance no further. It laps against it. Laps against it again and then three more times at the exact same point and then ten and then doesn't touch it on the next creep up and there! I think, that's the pivot point. I've marked it, seen it, can say with confidence it will come up no further today, that I've been here to witness the turning point. And then the water laps over the stick and lifts it, floats it a little further inland.

For my mother, the tumultuous sky and sea — and not any small figures she might sketch into the foreground — were characters to be reckoned with. She was the one who showed me in her paintings what she couldn't say in conversation: pay attention to what looms all around, however formless and blurred. For a long time I understood her focus as tutelage, spent years myself absorbed by landscapes blurred by ambiguity and mindscapes fogged by abstract notions of the spiritual. I seldom felt ungrounded, though one of the hazards of being engrossed by the groundless is that it's hard to tell when it's time to put more concrete and dirt — or stone — beneath the feet.

But there's a point — isn't there? — in most of our lives when we sense we've gone far enough and need to change direction. For so long I wanted the boundless out-there, wanted to lose myself in its mystery. And now, the opposite: absorption in these objects that litter the shore, ones I can rearrange or stash inside my pockets. Perhaps someday I'll know I don't have to choose between them, that it's possible to study the sea and the sky *and* to have a hand in arranging things, whether they're under the surface or exposed on top. Isn't this what Goldsworthy's paradoxes suggest? The tide's ancient rhythm, after all, is first to conceal and then to reveal.

And this one, it seems, hasn't turned yet. About so many things in our lives — obsessions, dogma, a daughter's unkind boyfriend — maybe the opposite of the Pueblos' belief is sometimes truer: if you scrutinize them, they won't change. Pivotal points might need a little darkness. In the house just up the bank, my husband and friends by now have probably lit the candles, poured the wine, begun to wonder if I'll come in in time for dinner. At my feet, the stick twirls again, but this time, I swear, the water doesn't quite cover it.

7

MEIOFAUNA, A HOLY MAN, AND SINGING SAND

Incoherence

A HALF HOUR AGO I GAVE UP trying to make a mental map of the souks of Marrakech, which are places not to be when your tolerance for the disorderly is low. Alleys and aisles intersect at odd angles; brasswear is displayed between caged iguanas and chess sets. Shoppers dressed in jellabas and turbans, speaking an utterly alien, guttural language, weave through this dizzying array of spice and appliance shops, shelves jammed with stoneware. I get swept along with them, unable to ask directions. I need a map that doesn't exist, at least here or there a sign. Is the metalworkers' section that way, up past that slipper shop? And what happened to the drum store whose location I'd memorized? Because beyond it, if you turn right and then left, lies what I'm already eager for — the wide open square full of sunshine and an easy walk to my hotel. Sometimes even the illusion of clarity is welcome, though an open space is, ipso facto, no more coherent than a cluttered one.

When I step sideways to get out of the crowd, I'm surrounded by shelves and hangers full of gorgeous scarves — paisleys and subtle stripes, oranges, turquoise, some long enough you could wrap your entire body in them, others meant to cover just the head. The merchant approaches. *You want to see?* I think he asks. And I nod, only because I need a break for a few minutes, to stand unbumped and still. He brings me a dozen, unfolds them on the counter, drapes them over my arm, and keeps up a steady stream of words — *madam, madam, you want to buy?* — that hums beneath the call-to-prayer broadcast from a nearby mosque and the babble of the crowd. Aware of cinnamon and urine, flowers and sweat, I sway between appreciation and annoyance. Smiling, he drapes three more scarves across the table, murmurs something, I guess, about the quality of color or weave. These, I choose, holding out two. I know I'm supposed to bargain, but suddenly it all seems to require so much effort. Too many decisions to make in a language not mine — catching a cab (how do I know what they're saying? Am I getting ripped off?), shopping, even eating (*you want mahchi or mqualli?*). I give the merchant a hundred dirham and after another hour in the mingle-mangle I'm out in the square, trying to figure out bus routes to the coast.

∾

On a quiet Moroccan beach the next day, I bypass a group of camels for hire and sit down in the white sand, let it run through my fingers like a comfortable ritual. Blake's famous line — "To see a World in a Grain of Sand" — occurs to me now, but the truth is, I've never understood it. I know the image is mystical and inspiring to many, a call to see the infinite in every miniscule bit of matter, but even if that were possible, it seems too reductive, too dismissive of the mishmash that — for better or worse — makes up most of our lives. To see the world *between* grains of sand, though, is actually doable and therefore more of a challenge.

For that, I'd need a microscope. And what I'd see when I peered through its lens is a hidden universe of mazelike spaces between the grains. They'd look like frost patterns on a windowpane, only they wouldn't be ice but a labyrinth of thread-thick corridors fractaling through the sand.

Negative space, artists call it. Clearance, I call it. The room between objects — breaks in cloud cover, holes in doilies, columns of air between balusters. Nothing visible happens there; the space looks empty. Though clearance doesn't necessarily mean clarity, without those slivers and dots of emptiness, there'd be no chance to see what is and isn't there. A doily would become a napkin, a poem would look on the page like prose, balustrades would appear as walls. The loosely woven grass roofs of the souks would seem like ceilings.

Madam, madam, you want to ride? a man interrupts, motioning toward his camel. *Ninety dirham, ninety dirham, a bargain,* he says. He's grinning and waving his hands; his enthusiasm seems to shrink my thinking, narrow my thoughts to this one exotic offer. Leaning closer, he nods his head — *yes, yes?* — and five minutes later I'm lurching on a camel in a line of camels, all of us ambling down the beach. The tourist in front of me looks gleeful; the one behind, tentative. I'm somewhere between surprised and intent on hanging on. The guide, it seems, between satisfied and back-at-work.

Below us, the spaces between grains shift and reconfigure but they never disappear because those gaps and clearances aren't liminal — on their way between one thing and another. They're interstitial, from Latin roots meaning *to stand between.* Not *pass* between, but *stand.* The word does not suggest transition, but occupancy.

Creatures live between those grains of sand. Every time this camel moves, it steps on millions of living things. I don't know whether some of them can feel above them another hoof about to thud, whether some get squashed while others flee to quieter crevices. But they'll survive, even flourish: stumpy tardigrades, segmented beach fleas, hook-mouthed Loricifera, algae grazers, slithering, flapping rotifers, creatures with suction toes, spear-wielding predators, and urn-looking things with medusa heads.

Meiofauna, they're called. In a mere handful of sand, thousands of them, invisible, brainless, hungry. Under the press of camel hooves and human feet, jeep tires and tide, they thrive between the grains in tiny tunnels and mite-sized spaces. Jammed next to other shifting grains, jut to jut, angle to corner, the grains still create plenty of crooked hallways and low-ceilinged tunnels to slither through. If the sand is young — unpolished, rough-cut — the angular grains will nestle less closely, leaving more room for the creatures to maneuver through.

High up on my camel, I like to picture them down there, employing various strategies for navigating through their mazes. A gastrotrich, for example, lugs around a dual cement-gland contraption. To get from one grain to the next, it uses one gland to secrete a drop of cement, which affixes the creature momentarily to the granule and allows it to pull itself forward. The other gland then secretes a dissolver, which unsticks the paste, allowing it to reach for the next hold — a tiny swinging Tarzan, gluing and then ungluing itself to an underground string of grains.

Or there's the kinorhynch, whose name derives from Greek (*motion* plus *snout*) to mean *movable snout.* It's capable of retracting its entire head into its own body, a strategy that we introverts envy. A kinorhynch navigates between the grains by ramming its head like a grappling iron into a grain and then pulling its body after it. Some of the meiofauna swing the exopods on their antennae in a modified butterfly stroke against the sand. Others glide and undulate. A few have hooked mouths and claws they sink into granules, miniature climbers with crampons, only these aren't rock walls they're clinging to but individual particles.

Suddenly, my camel stops and stands, legs slightly splayed, nose in the air. Camel contempt, some have labeled its haughty smirk. It chews its cud and refuses to move. Behind us, another camel nears so close its guide has to jerk it to a halt. Its rider — another American — lurches forward and my guide erupts in a steady stream of what sounds like cursing. Beneath the camel's supercilious gaze, he tugs on the rope and dodges an arc of spit and — out of nowhere — I think again of a photograph of an Indian holy man who's buried himself up to his neck. His Hindu devotees have packed sand around his legs, torso, and arms, brushed loose grains from his face, strewn flowers under his chin. In the photograph, the only thing visible is his head, which looks as if it's been cut off. The caption says he intends to stay entombed like this for ten days, that he believes being buried to the chin will deepen his meditation.

Who knows where such random images come from, what prompts the intrusion of disconnected thoughts, or why we want to drift in them awhile. I allow the picture to linger: his body, upright and immobile in its straitjacket of packed sand, the weight of what surrounds him pressing in. Whatever air pockets might have formed at his armpits, between his legs, must have been filled as the sand above settled down. He has five feet of sand on top of his insteps. If he tries to move his hand a couple of inches, he'll be pushing sideways under thirty inches of pressure. The grains must be packed between his ankles, his thighs, against his belly, pinning his arms to his side. And between all those grains: millions of meiofauna. Rummaging around five feet below the surface, slipping between grains, whirring through miniscule tunnels, climbing across granules, they'll find his feet, his legs; they'll burrow and poke, test out their sucking mouth parts. A man can't go that long without eliminating body waste. They'll find that too.

He won't feel them, of course, and besides, he's probably less interested in the spaces between grains than in the spaces between thoughts. Meditation, after all, is another attempt at clearance, the kind that can reveal certain clarities or, more likely, how muddled our thinking often is. Unruly mind, I've often thought when I've tried to meditate. One thought bombards another, a third veers in from who-knows-where; they pile up and begin to knot and meanwhile, there I am on my cushion, not even trying to follow one thought or another but to clear them out, make a little room. But for what? More thoughts, it seems. And sure enough, they keep coming — would I really want them not to? — until I'm reminded how hard-won a moment of real clarity can be.

In an Indian village once, not far from where the holy man's head lay exposed above the ground, I wandered one night and saw too much. I knew the protocol — you keep your eyes forward and respect the privacy of those small rooms that open right on the alley. Fresh cooking smells wafted from the windows — spices I couldn't name, chicken, some kind of greens. It was hot. A door was ajar. I looked in. A child scuttled across the concrete floor. His skinny legs were splayed and bent so that his calves seemed glued to the backs of his thighs. He'd learned to use his hands and drag his folded legs behind him. He moved fast, out of sight, and instantly a woman filled the doorway, sari snapping. She shook the spoon in her hand at me and let loose a stream of Hindi I didn't understand and yet I did.

How, I want to ask the holy man's head, are we to make any sense of scenes like that? And how, if the world presses close while our meditation deepens, do we know whether we're reducing distractions or sloughing off what's hard to look at? I admire tranquility in people until I see it's the result of denial. Serenity's easy, after all, if you don't pay attention to anything but what's serene.

I don't know what the holy man felt when he emerged — insouciance? disregard? deepened empathy? disembodiment? — or whether the meditation changed how he understood the fortunes and misfortunes of the world. At its best, meditation clears room in the mind so that awareness of everything is heightened. Including, I would hope, what we don't always see: not meiofauna, necessarily, but hunger, hardship, disharmony. At its worst, it deepens a dangerous passivity.

Hsst, the guide urges again. Camels can be stubborn — bored, it seems — with humans who pay money to ride around on their backs. When it begins at last to move, he leads it — and me — up a dune between bunches of beach grass. It seems wrong, in some ways, to be carried here. Perhaps more than any other terrain, we know a beach by how it feels beneath our feet — damp or dry, yielding or firm. And sometimes by how it sounds. When we were children, our parents used to take us to Singing Beach just north of Boston. I'm sure they laid out blankets, opened an umbrella, pulled sandwiches and cold drinks from a bag, but mostly I remember the sound of the sand—a squeak, like dental floss between crowded teeth or two pieces of taffeta rubbed together—and that we could change it with every step: speed it up if we ran, slow it down if we walked, sustain it for a moment if we twisted the balls of our feet in a jitterbug version of sand dancing. I didn't care then about how or why the sound occurred, didn't make up stories about subterranean music or sand monsters moaning underfoot.

Others have.

Marco Polo described it as musical instruments. Tribal folks in desert camps heard it as dark activity in the upper reaches of the underworld. Still others believed the sound thrums up from the sand-muffled bell towers of monasteries buried deep in the dunes. Darwin heard it in Brazil every time his horse put his foot down in the sand. "A chirping noise," he claimed. Singing dunes—just thirty-five of them in the world—sing louder than singing beaches. They thunder and drum, mimic sirens.

Sand can make music because, unlike snow or mud, sand is incoherent. Its grains cannot cohere. You can't make cohesive sand patties, the way you can make snowballs or mudpies, because the grains cannot cling together. No matter how tightly you pack them, they won't stick to other grains, flatten or soften, lose their discreteness. Even as it blows across a beach or sinks beneath a camel's hoof, every grain retains its shape.

When those grains are silica-laced and a certain size, they collide with other particles just below the surface at a rate of about one hundred times a second, setting off an array of standing waves. In a kind of feedback loop, the waves begin to reinforce each other and then synchronize the collisions, producing stronger vibrations which are then magnified by the upper layer of the beach or dune. But before—or is it beyond?—the physics lies the mystery of incoherence and music. Foghorns and trombones, some have claimed. Monster harps.

There've been times when I've been concerned with incoherence of a different kind. Anyone who's ever graded a freshman's paper knows that if you can't string two ideas together you also probably can't make a reasonable case for why it's sometimes necessary to live with contradictions. "Incoherent!" I used to scribble on my students' papers. I'd try to get them to connect the thoughts. "How does this idea follow from the previous one?" I wanted them to think lucidly, to link one part of an argument to another. "Contrast?" I'd ask them. "Or analogy? Do you need *however* or *similarly*? Maybe *most importantly*?" I still value such careful thinking, of course, but I'm also aware that there've been times when I, in the midst of untangling a story, couldn't have said a thing about graceful transitions.

I can't now, either. What, after all, do meiofauna, a holy man's head, and singing sand really have to do with one another? Reminders, I have to admit, that beneath this trio of current fascinations there's no thread that connects them, makes of them some seamless whole. It's hard, it seems, to keep ourselves from looking for unifying metaphors or to admit that such willful looking often results in contrived connections and distorted descriptions.

Harder, still, to know that even if we think we've found coherence in a certain chaos, that doesn't necessarily help us live with it. Narrating the shifts among contradictions, after all, is not the same as occupying them. During those phases in my life when I've felt awkwardly lurched between incongruities — one parent and the other, intimacy and solitude, what I said and what I felt — I often fashioned metaphors — that notion of music, say, emerging from the incoherence of sand — as omens of hope. And though I wouldn't deny the power of hope — it can inspire patience, if nothing else — such metaphors, I know now, can artificially sweeten the discord, bail us out of the present. An understandable wish, though in the long run Keats's claim is oddly more consoling: "There is nothing stable in the world; uproar's your only music."

There's no map to the souks, no map to the mind. On some days we're left with looking at the world through the lens of incoherence. A lot of things don't make sense, and often seeing clearly has less to do with searching for coherence and more to do with accepting the disconnected, unwieldy disparities that surround us. Interstitial, I remind myself again, not liminal. What would it take to *occupy* that space between incongruities? To not hurry through it? Sometimes the only cure for the angst of incoherence is to make a little room for it.

Meanwhile, atop the small dune thirty feet from the high-tide line, my camel stops again and looks down its long nose at the guide. Haughty or bored? Neither, I realize. It seems, in fact, that I've been riding the most bemused-looking animal in the world whose behavior I now imagine as commentary — on the guide, his job, maybe even my own desire to make meaning out of grains of sand. When it spits toward my guide, he curses, and I watch the saliva arc and then moisten the grains, wonder whether a tardigrade has just rammed into a suddenly sodden wall and been forced to change direction.

8 WENTLETRAP

The Pleasures of Aversions

> Objects are permitted inside our veil of privacy, which
> makes them intimate . . . and possibly obscene.
>
> — TIM McCREIGHT

THE SHELL IN MY HAND is less than an inch long and looks like
a spiral staircase. Or a tiny board-and-batten cone carved out of
marble, twisted and then cinched every quarter of an inch. Close
to pure white, its beauty is almost enough to make me forget that
inside something repulsive might still be alive: a visceral mass, gelatinous blob, creature an X-ray would reveal as boneless. That the
intricate spires and turbans and perfectly concentric whorls strewn
on beaches all over the world were created by such things complicates my praise. I'm drawn to the goop of a swamp and interested
in scat of all kinds, but there are days, like this one, when I tire of
marvel. The truth is, I can't stand leeches or sea cucumbers, even
the garden slugs that slime the stone paths at home. How slippery
can my standards be?

This isn't moral disgust, of course, which I feel, say, toward
Edmund Wilson — all his arrogant, alcoholic binges! — but which
doesn't negate my appreciation of his brilliant critical work. It's a
visceral repugnance, a recoiling aversion to the snail's shell-less
body. I doubt that it could do anything this morning — make an
even more beautiful shell or wipe up its own slime — to soften my
attitude. I won't even touch a creature that hasn't a bit of bone to
press against. They seem like errant body parts, slugs like thick

albino lips gliding sideways down the sidewalk on the skim on their own glisten. A lost piece of intestine, aimless without its ileum. The embodiment of what would happen if we went around spilling our guts and they came to life at night without us, slouched on dark street corners in bleary, beery talk with anyone who'd listen. My repulsion must have something to do with the fact that snails have eyeballs. And they move. They have this foot that ripples over its own carpet of mucous. Of course I want their shells all emptied, the insides scoured, even sterilized. Who could stand that mucilaginous ooze gliding up their arm?

But living or dead, this one in my hand commands my attention and so the challenge today is to find something in its slimy life that I might possibly admire. Here's a feat: A gastropod begins its life as a glutinous bag of organs draped by a mantle whose function is to extract calcium and carbon dioxide from the sea and transform them into calcium carbonate crystals. Not an easy task, think I, who have trouble absorbing enough calcium for my bones. It makes some of its crystals prism-shaped, embedded with proteid molecules, and exudes them in variously oriented layers. They interlock, harden into a shell that can then pucker into ridges and flutes, spread out in fans, elongate into tusks. Some are impressively iridescent, purple-stained, spun into spiny jewel boxes, rose-petaled butterfly shells. Infinite forms, intricate and graceful and ridiculously excessive. To what end? I finally want to know. Why this gaudy conglomeration of shapes and colors and ornamentation?

If a snail had consciousness and access to a mirror, I'd understand its need to mask its boneless, vacant face with exterior fluff and frills. I've known folks like that, been one at times myself, drawers and closets full of what finally couldn't do the trick. But perhaps I'm being unkind. In *The Wound and the Bow,* after all, that same Edmund Wilson shrewdly claims that Philoctetes' isolation, caused by his festering wound and its perpetual stench, contributed to character, gave him a kind of nobility and years of practice with his bow, a chance to perfect his art. Haven't many of us done likewise? Transformed the pain of loneliness or violation into something interesting if not artful? Think of Caravaggio, Anne Frank, or Frida Kahlo, perhaps even my own mother. No, about snails, I'm being much too generous. They haven't, of course, an ounce of self and therefore no sense of others' repulsion, no need at all for beauty, no need for anything, I suspect, except to satisfy their hungers.

I think this one in my hand might be a wentletrap. The size and spirals look about right. Hungry and at sea, wentletraps like to eat anemones. They latch on and secrete a pink anesthetic. The anemone goes numb, cannot feel its own juices being sucked up through the snail's proboscis. Whelks, much larger than wentletraps, don't care for anemones and search instead for small streams of siphoned water spouting from buried clams. The streams are often invisible to us, but the whelk can follow one to its source. It seizes the tightly closed clam in its foot and uses its own big shell as a hammer. Some small snails barge right through the aperture of a larger one, ooze up the coiled shell to where their prey has backed its pustule self against its own shell wall, and wave their radula tongues, which in some species contain a quarter of a million teeth. In Hawaii, a cone snail flits its harpoonlike tongue so fiercely it'll pierce a scuba diver's glove and inject a paralyzing drug. They all do this, without expression, eyes on the ends of their tentacles incapable of blinking, mouths not much more than a hole in the visceral hump that rides the thick, sticky foot.

All right, I'll try again to admire. Here's another wonder: Snails undergo an engineering marvel called internal torsion. When a snail is in its free-floating larval state, a tiny blob in the water, its mouth is at one end and its anus is, sensibly, at the other. Sustenance enters here, waste exits there, and there's little chance of it fouling its own food. But such an arrangement affords little chance of growing a shell it can both carry around and hide inside. The center of gravity would be too high; it'd be forever toppling over, leaving the snail on its side in the sand, its foot rooting around in the air for a surface to glide on.

So, early in its development, the snail rearranges its insides, twisting its visceral mass 180 degrees. Imagine taking a wide, cooked noodle, laying it flat on the kitchen counter, and then sliding the two ends toward each other so that a hump forms in the middle. Then swing the right end around in a semicircle away from you, toward the other end, letting the hump twist toward you until you've got the right end square on top of the left. In snail equivalency, you've just moved the anus from the rear and positioned it on top of the head. Now its rudimentary shell, which rotated in the process like a periscope, can more easily coil, making it easier for the snail to carry and withdraw into.

And the problem of dumping its own waste on its head? This potential design flaw interests me. It'd be like having the upstairs apartment discharge its sewer out the window above your balcony, providing a constant supply of scat to study for hints of diet and migratory patterns. But the snail evidently has less interest in feces than I do. It perfectly positions a certain slit in its shell, shoots the stuff out away from its mouth, and becomes one of the most evolutionarily successful creatures on the planet: more than thirty thousand species, outnumbered only by insects. Their pale, boneless bodies have infiltrated almost every beach, most shallow waters, mud flats, and wharfs, inched up flower stalks in backyard gardens, slid silently out over the broad leaves of neighborhood trees. One kind weighs thirty pounds, some live for twenty-five years, a few have been observed dragging fifty times their own weight, and the body of each of them is comprised mostly of that visceral hump and flat, creeping sole.

It's winter on the Jersey shore, and the landscape's a muted cinder and buff, seaweed well worn, the waves seeming to do what they do out of long habit. They come in, they drop their load, drag bits of the wrack line back out to sea. Boredom, I sometimes think, is what the unprejudiced suffer. No biases to break up equanimity, no impulsive judgments, just the suspended calm of acceptance, the flattened waiting for the facts. A good enough reason, I conclude today, to opt for the opposite because abhorrence at least prompts some kind of action, while appreciation inspires only praise. Isn't it true we're often more active about the things that we dislike? They prick our own precious wounds, which move back onto center stage, take up the limelight once more. Beauty, as Simone Weil suggests, requires us "to give up our imaginary position as the center" and puts us in the audience again, silent except for applause. But ugliness does the opposite: recenters us in the middle of our prejudices and tests our compassion as beauty never does.

Clearly, I have failed. It's untoward, I know, for a naturalist to rant like this about revulsion. In a different mood, on a different day, I might have seen the thing in a better light. Perhaps I should apologize. But to whom? The snail itself? Without even a rudimentary ear in that pulpy end that passes for a head, it can't hear a single thing. And besides, did I mention the way some of them court? They sniff out the slime trail of a potential mate whom they greet in a long, mucousy foot version of a handshake and caress with those bulbous eye stalks until each suddenly impales the other's gelatinous foot with a calcerous love dart. Who could possibly love that? And about this snail still in my hand? Absent compassion, is there nothing today that would soften my take on this slimy creature? Ah yes, a little garlic, perhaps, with some herbed butter and a glass of white wine.

9   LIME SEA GLASS
Transformations

> He had said that everything possessed
> The power to transform itself, or else,
> And what meant more, to be transformed.
>
> — WALLACE STEVENS

GIVEN THE HYPE, Glass Beach is not at first glance a hopeful place. The rocks and surf of the northern California coast are magnificent, of course, but the site doesn't seem much different from hundreds of other such rugged spots, and, besides, I've come not for beauty but to see how the ocean can transform human carelessness.

Glass Beach has its origins in ignominy. For almost twenty years in the middle of the twentieth century, people backed their pickups to the edge of the cliff next to the small town of Fort Bragg, California, set the emergency brake, climbed into the bed of the truck, and hurled household refuse — ironing boards, lamps, kitchen tables — into the Pacific Ocean. Those with less heft to their heave must have seen the trash bounce off the sloping cliff on its way down, the electric cords whipping like lassos, toasters careening off the rocks, tin cans somersaulting down. Others might have watched the arc an old radio makes, the way the brown plastic casing flies apart and then sinks out of sight.

It didn't stop with metal and plastic junk. The people of the town and nearby communities also pitched a lot of glass over the cliff edge I can see just ahead. I imagine turning back the clock and speeding up the film to watch a twenty-year cascade of beer bottles and sugar bowls, crystal figurines and picture frames, bud vases, cracked wine glasses, burnt-out light bulbs, old shower doors and candle holders disappearing into the sea that stretches out below me. I peer over the edge of the cliff, but there's no sign down there of trash or rubble. No sign, either, of anything the Glass Beach brochures had described: "Dazzling! Sparkles like jewels! Polished into gems!" Below me, waves lap as they do and the sand looks like ordinary sand.

Double-checking the directions I've been given, I retrace my steps and follow what might have once been a narrow road sloping toward the sea. Assuring me I'd be amazed, the motel clerk had handed me a map and drawn a small *x* on a crescent of beach that should by now be just twenty feet ahead. I'm expecting a swath of shimmer and glint, a kind of emptied pirate's chest strewn along the edge of the water. Instead, a few iris-looking plants, vivid purple-blue, sway a bit in the breeze between me and the sand. Ahead, mostly what I've seen on so many coastal postcards: beach taupes and tans, gray-brown rocks, and the blue water beyond. I check the map again.

A young woman walks toward me, headed back into town. I ask her and she turns, points directly at what lies just ahead. *That's it,* she says. *But you have to be closer. Keep going. And keep looking down.* Underfoot, asphalt turns to grit and then to sand, and fifty feet up the beach, a dog digs furiously while what shoots up, fountainlike, from between his paws isn't sand. It doesn't spray like sand does and it doesn't fall in wet clumps or tiny dunes. It rattles and clinks. Doll-sized doubloons, I fancy, walking toward him, or merely pebbles?

Neither. When I bend down and look closely, finally see them, they're everywhere. Chunks of opal, splinters of green, specks of cobalt blue. The amber ones glow like globs of something vital. Held up to the sun, they turn to honey. Balanced on a white piece, they become butterscotch, caramel. Some are a quarter inch across, some as large as earlobes, a few like flattened lima beans. Resisting the urge to dig, I pick them up and put them back, one at a time.

Thirty years after the town of Fort Bragg closed the beach to dumping, the transformed past began to wash ashore. It came, though, not as knife-edged shards or bits of glass that could slit a wrist, not as anything recognizable. Instead, these thousands of well-rubbed bits, their edges so smoothly polished I couldn't cut myself if I wanted to. Neither could any of the half-dozen people up and down the beach, digging with their hands or small shovels. They aren't wandering, the way people so often do along shorelines, stopping now and then to bend, turn over a shell, pocket it or not, and walk on. Working a dozen yards apart from each other, these folks kneel or sit, lower their fingers into the sand, as if they have something in mind that has nothing to do with a beachcomber's idle pleasures. Three of them, in blue jeans and sweatshirts, look to be in their twenties or thirties, too young to have owned anything that's now washing up along this shore. About the others, I'm less certain. Of course they can't expect to recognize a thing. A shattering impact and then time and the pressure of the sea would have altered texture and shape. Still, they seem to expect something. Most of us don't come to the shore, any shore, believing there's a chance that what's disappeared will be returned on the next tide. But at Glass Beach, something from the polluted past *is* coming back, and somehow it's been changed. Perhaps that's the secret hope: that if the flotsam of our lives must reappear it will be smoothed and softened into something promising.

Picking up a knuckle-sized bit of clear glass, I try to picture it before it shattered; I multiply its mass by a hundred, shape it into something recognizable — a goblet, a vase. It might have come from a local JCPenney, which bought it from a wholesaler who bought it from a glass-making factory where thousands of such containers were rolled out every week. I have long loved the art of extrapolation and its assumption that an imaginatively reassembled pile of fragments can suggest something unbroken. There's a certain comfort in following the clues, an expectation of coherence across time, as when an archaeologist finds a chunk of iron beneath a shredded basket and reconstructs in his head a village, a smithy, and a kitchen full of bread. Is this always the temptation with debris? To try to see it whole, before it broke into smithereens? That blue one there might have been the bottom of a cobalt vase on some dreamy woman's dresser. And that milky white one, an ashtray full of butts in a shag-carpeted living room with a couple who've forgotten how to talk with one another.

When I blur my eyes, the bits of glass all around me seem to retreat, to sink back into sand. The beach turns taupe again. When I get down on my hands and knees and look closely, they re-emerge, small pointillist dollops from a painter's brush. Though it isn't the only green on the beach — seaweed lies tangled in driftwood and algae slimes the rocks — it's a bright green bit of glass that interests me most. It seems both solid and luminescent. Heineken? A bottle of Coke?

Back even further: before it was glass, the glass was sand. Forget the "dust thou art, to dust returnest" of my childhood days full of Longfellow poems and Bible stories. Perhaps when it comes to inanimate things, *Sand thou was, to sand returnest,* is the less ignoble fate. Unlike dust, sand at least has a certain weight to it, the discreteness of separate grains. You can isolate a granule, hold it on the tip of your finger, wonder how long it will take it to break down even further. A hundred years from now, will anyone walking along Glass Beach even know which of the millions of granules here have had a different life? Some in the furnaces of humankind, gracing their tables, falling out of favor. Others, never touched by human hand, crumbling from mountain stone to rubble to pebbles and then sand. If no more glass washes ashore and the surf continues to pound what's already here, I doubt anyone in the future will be able to tell the difference. We'd need, then, not just an archaeologist here but a philosopher or two to tackle the question of how much alteration a thing can undergo and still be what it was.

We'd need a novelist too, someone to decide how much of the past we need to know to understand how someone or something has changed. In the case of this lime green chunk, it doesn't matter to me whether it once held Heineken or Coke. I'm more interested in the immutability of its color, the way it reflects light and quickens my imagination: "Green door," the old song goes, "what's that secret you're keepin'?"

∾

On the other side of the continent, near a glassblower's studio on a Maine island, an artist has hung an old wooden gate in the middle of a forest. It's not a well-traveled place; there's no building there, no suggestion of paddock or yard, just a gate of wooden planks suspended between two pines. If you're out for a hike and chance upon it, you can, of course, go around it. It's easy walking there, the ground all needled and soft, no reason for a path, certainly no reason for a gate. But the artist, by setting the object in an unexpected context, has transformed the ordinary, and every time I'm there I'm seduced. I want to open that gate and step through whatever invisible portal it defines. A made object in the middle of the natural, it becomes the thing, as Wallace Stevens says in "Anecdote of the Jar," that makes "the slovenly wilderness / Surround that hill." Put a gate or small article in the midst of an otherwise wilderness and suddenly the eye is differently engaged.

Here on the Pacific coast, the sea's panorama and untidy beach in full vista-view, the lime green fragment is becoming more than artifact. It's beginning to work as an agent of perception, inviting the imagination to participate. Without that participation, the coast is lovely, yes, with the subtle rusty hues of tidal pools, the leather-slime of kelp and curling pound-plash of surf, but sometimes clear seeing has less to do with observing what's visible and more to do with transforming what's incomplete.

This clear, triangular shard in my hand — vase? goblet? who

knows its history? — reminds me of a cutter I once knew, a girl named Carla who opened slits in her thigh with broken glass. The point wasn't suicide, she said later. The point was that physical pain could alter emotional pain. A corner of the glass would press in, dimple the skin until it split. She used the point of a pen to show me. She never went deep. I always saw her in summer, in short sleeves, long pants, quiet in the back corner of the arts camp, capable of writing a line I worried about confronting. I imagined the scars beneath her jeans. By the time she was eighteen, she'd moved away from a family that had almost destroyed her, discarded the glass, begun to write whole pages of lines I still hesitated to question, until she insisted that I deal with her poem and not the life that triggered it. *Is it working?* she'd ask. And while I'd be worrying about trauma, she'd go on to prompt me: *The line, the sounds? How about that image at the end of the stanza?* I learned from her that a poem — perhaps any artifact — not bound to its origins can become something that matters less for the situation it represents and more for what it — tough, resilient, lenslike — *does,* which is to rearrange the past and make possible a larger question, something perhaps about complicity, maybe forgiveness.

∾

My digging sneaker uncovers a white piece that looked exactly like a gummy bear. I put it between my teeth and bite down slowly. The instant shiver down the spine is like fingernails on a chalkboard. I've barely grazed glass to enamel, but it's enough to add those two elements to the long list I've kept since I was twelve: things that must never touch each other. *Pansies and quartz. Clouds and peat moss. My mother's blush brush and turpentine.* I don't know the origin of this need to name the things that seem incongruous, nor do I understand the logic of my choices. I can recall no nightmares of flowers shattering the insides of stones, nothing surreal, no childhood catastrophes resulting from the "collision of the incompatibles," as I later called it. My tendency seems, instead, to have to do with the grating, for example, of red against pink or the chafe of steel against dandelion fluff. Do such things offend some latent aesthetic sensibility, the way our third-grade teacher whispered *ouch* if one of us showed up in a plaid skirt and checkered blouse? Or do they represent a different kind of clash, as in a Magritte painting? *Ouch*, that third-grade teacher might have said about his work, which depends on the odd juxtaposition of often ordinary objects — a steam engine, for example, emerging from a fireplace — to suggest plasticity. Is that what my list might be about? An early, unconscious obsession with the interpenetrating and improbable worlds Magritte's painting can suggest?

Where Magritte might have painted a mirror as a squid's head with an apple inside, I imagine, instead, a mirror hurled off the Fort Bragg cliff, shattering on impact, a shower of clear shards cascading through water, and a school of rockfish just below, their sudden need to weave, as if through a 3-D slalom course made of falling glass. And what about the bottom? The giant anemone lives in these parts. An animal that looks like a green underwater version of the red bee balm that grows in my garden, it's among the largest: seven inches wide, nearly a foot tall. Because it can live for decades, it's conceivable that in the waters just offshore, beneath the cliff, some creatures remain from the middle of the last century. Imagine them: their tentacles — emerald green and delicate — waving in the currents, searching for mussels and shrimp they can swoosh into their mouths, while fifty feet above, a cracked mirror plummets toward the rock to which one anemone has firmly attached itself. If it had eyes that could look upward, it might have seen its own image careening toward it in the moments before death, a green-tentacled double, dive-bombing from above. There's no chance a sea anemone could use such a mishap to paint its own version of a Magritte, to adopt a new religion, or to practice evasive maneuvers, and no way to know how long it took for that shard-glittered, sharp-edged ocean floor to soften, become less a menace to small suction feet and bottom-cruising crabs.

Each inexorable push and pull of tide over the next fifty years shoved the bits of glass a little forward and then back, scraped them across the bottom. The sea with its suspended particles, its stone and sandy shores, acts like a giant rock polisher. It tumbles and scours, abrades and chafes, finally burnishes and buffs. We know now that what's discarded doesn't disappear and that what's in friction with the world — and what, including us, is not? — can be both shattered and smoothed.

Offshore, a fishing boat churns along the horizon, and closer in, the waves continue to pound. Everything here is tossed or rolled — driftwood, rocks, seaweed — in meaningless patterns, an untidy scene. Against a rock, a strand of bullwhip kelp, nine feet long, and next to it, a swarm of flies above a glob of damp and thready seaweed. Meanwhile, five people on the beach have become nine and then a dozen. They're crouched and digging, or standing and toeing. So am I. I clench the lime shard. *Green Door* keeps running through my head: "what's that secret you're keepin'?" Do any of us expect to find anything valuable? "The answer we need now," the *I Ching* says, "will be found if we allow ourself to be led through the small door of the improbable." Out here, beach to the north, the south, the sea all the way to Japan, it's the improbable thing in my hand that both focuses and complicates my thought.

ॐ

My husband and I and two close friends have been talking for years about transformation. One of us doesn't believe in it. One of us is a clear example of it, and all of us love to argue about transformation's promise and delusions. We're thinking, I suppose, about our own habits of indifference or recklessness, and what we've discarded — not just other people but parts of ourselves — and whether it's ever possible to radically vary one's temperament or character. The more ubiquitous evidence is that change in human behavior is minute and incremental. Dramatic change, I suspect, is most often the result of an unwilled collision of two consciousnesses within a single person. Is that also the origin of art: the collision and resulting paradox?

I put the white piece on a rock and empty my pockets, arrange dozens of glass bits in a tight circle, a small Tiffany lampshade disassembled and rearranged with that chunk of lime in the center. I came to Glass Beach to see what happens when humans foul an ocean. I thought the story had to do with carelessness — and it does — but I'm reminded that a thing can outlive, maybe even transcend, its history, be returned to us years later, softened and small, as a mosaic of color-bits finally ripe for rearrangement.

Purified, one woman claims. She's headed up the beach for the second time in two days, she says. From a city somewhere, she's come solely for the glass. *A jeweler?* I ask. There's a whole business, I know, that fashions sea glass into necklaces, earrings, brooches.

No, she replies. *I put them on my altar.*

She's not Catholic or Hindu, nothing like that, she tells me. She wants around her the small signs of the sanctified. The sea can do that, she insists, can take something broken and redeem it.

Too old to put much stake in purity, I back away from the rock with its tiny green slab in the center, more impenetrable and more inviting than the panorama of the sea and its froth, long beach and translucent fog. That bit of glass represents both carelessness and hope. The place was once trashed, after all, but the resulting glass seems to please at least the people here: beachcombers and artists and those of us amazed by how the sea's natural forces seem to have altered human carelessness. Without consciousness, of course, there's nothing moral about the sea's forgiveness — as there would be, or should be, for us. But that doesn't lessen — in fact it might heighten — my appreciation of what the beach has subtly become.

A wave sloshes toward me, clear, carrying, apparently, nothing. No shell, no seaweed strand, no color-glisten I can see. It spreads its froth out along the sand, sinks, and seems to retreat. The beach looks unchanged, though I know now not to trust that appearance. If there is such a thing as transformation, perhaps the smaller manifestation is often the more reliable. Perhaps if we're lucky, we might salvage the small or unrecognizable as an agent of perception, the thing that prompts the imagination to focus and funnel, to be the lime door we might occasionally walk through, the trigger, finally, to some larger question.

10 BOTTLE AND FEATHER
A Different Question

RECUPERATING FROM A HEART ATTACK in St. Petersburg, Florida, the beach just two blocks away, my mother takes long naps. From her bedroom door, I watch the steady rise and fall of the blankets, or I curl on her couch and doze while she does. Sometimes I slip out the door. Today, though, the sea's usual *come hither* and *beware* seem an irregular romp of arrhythmic waves with none of the usual lure. The water is gray here, the beach trafficked by terns and gulls, shells everywhere. And what's left of Icarus, I muse, picking up a long white feather.

Who knows why I want to imagine him this late afternoon, far from the beaches I usually wander. Maybe because I wonder what it would have been like to have parents who know their children well enough to fashion the metaphoric wings best suited for their flights. Or maybe because I never behaved like Icarus and wish I sometimes had: a kid so full of the thrill he ignored his father's plea to stay close by him, and went past his limits — too high and then too low while his father touched safely down in Sicily.

A part of me wonders, though, whether in the end — maze or no maze — such dramatic departures disrupt any more than does a quiet slipping out the door. After all, in the most famous painting of the myth — Brueghel's *The Fall of Icarus* — nobody notices the fall at all. A plowman keeps plowing the field, a man tends his sheep, a ship sails right by the boy's legs flailing above his underwater, upside-down torso whose lungs by then must be filling with water. Nobody even pauses. "About suffering they were never wrong," Auden writes in his poem about the painting; "it takes place / While someone else is eating or opening a window or just walking dully along."

Perhaps that's what I'm doing too, picking up bits of tidal debris, toying with them as objects set against a background I have yet to find. Without a frame, few of us know what we're supposed to look at or what's been left out of the picture. Nobody ever mentions Icarus's mother, for example, and in Brueghel's painting, there's no sign of his famous father either. Instead, Brueghel's interested in how we ignore or turn from disaster, resume our ordinary lives. He's arranged his painting in response to that question.

And though Auden also evokes the implications of indifference, he, too, excluded Daedalus from his poem. Humanity's apathy, it seems to me this particular afternoon, can be turned into art that chills, but when it comes to individual loss, we're on our own. There's no frame or form for me today, no painterly eye here to crop and arrange what I feel, just a wind off the ocean and nothing visible to the west for miles, a gallery-less world where the best I can do is to try and caption it:

Girl with Feather Considers Icarus

Woman Whose Mother Is Usually Elsewhere

Woman on the Beach Knows That an Invisible Freighter Has Just Run Aground.

For me, one of the old lures of feathers and shells has always been that they had nothing to do with human stories, had most likely never been touched by human hands. Remnants of lives utterly indifferent to ours, they helped me imagine a balance to the often too-intimate mess and fray of our emotional lives. Today, though, that remove seems insufficient. I want to rearrange them, make something of them. These sand dollars, for example, should be stacked with others and photographed against an up-ended dory.

A half hour more, I figure, maybe a half mile, before she wakes up and I need to cook us a meal. A still life, I think: *Scallops on Fine China,* then *A Spray of Beach Grass next to Capsules of Coumadin.* And then my foot kicks a half-buried bottle, the kind that once held Chablis or chardonnay. Its cork is algae-encrusted, surface murky with sea scum. I dig it out, brush off the sand. Inside, something pale and long.

From where this sudden feeling of foreboding? My heart skips and immediately the old argument with self begins: it's just a bottle that's floated here. I know I'm projecting onto it my current worries, making it more than it is. We sometimes do this — don't we? — when we're eager or desperate for signs we're not alone. But if I yield to this foreboding and try to lob it back, it won't sail more than thirty feet into the sea — I failed every softball-throwing test ever invented. Most likely it will float in again before I can make it off the beach. And besides, it's ridiculous, I know — as if an anonymous bottle-tosser or the sea itself could give a hoot about what's brought me here to this beach today.

No, Brueghel's right, at least about our individual angst: it takes place while others carry on, while they do what they do. I watch a sandpiper chase a receding wave like a wind-up toy. A man rubs lotion onto the skin of a small boy's arms. A teenage boy, arms flailing, skim-boards past a group of smirking girls. A woman toys with a feather and beached bottle while her mother's heart is laboring a few blocks away.

She's awake when I return, sitting in the living room. *Look,* I show her. *And something's inside.*

Washed, the bottle's pale green, uncracked. Somebody has sealed the cork with paraffin. I can't begin to budge it.

Put it in the window, she suggests, *and raise the blinds.*

Sunlit, it turns almost emerald. Inside, a dry, rolled piece of paper is clearly visible.

What do you think? she asks. *A note? Who would've sent it?*

I try again to get the cork off. *We could break the glass,* I propose.

No, no, she says. *Put it back by the window.*

It gleams there like a tinted glow stick, the kind cavers take underground.

She bets it's from a man who needs to be rescued from some island. I guess a sailor about to go down with his ship. No, she speculates, how about a woman on the English shore looking for her soul mate. We're speaking playfully. And not. Back and forth we do this over dinner — *Mother and Daughter Try to Talk to Each Other in Code* — until she tires and retreats to bed.

Dreamers do heave bottles into the water, as do pranksters and jilted lovers ("Darling, come home"). Some bottles have traveled from Puerto Rico to Belize, Mexico to the Philippines, survived the ravages of seawater and sun, circulated for more than twenty years, and carried all kinds of notes:

One, from near the site of a downed aircraft: "All is lost."

Another: "To my wife — Wherever you are, I'll always be with you."

One that said in scrawled handwriting: "I love you all." Signed, *Jesus Christ.*

Though many of them might be jokes, others originate with researchers studying ocean currents. A teacher in Hawaii, for example, has tossed close to a thousand bottles, each of them with a note asking the finder to contact the school. They weren't a joke to Queen Elizabeth either, who, in the sixteenth century, reportedly appointed an official "Uncorker of Ocean Bottles" and proclaimed that, under penalty of death, no one but he be permitted to open them.

The rationale had to do with the British navy using the bottles to send messages ashore, but, researchers and espionage aside, the urge, I suspect, has more to do with imagining that there might be a perfect listener out there who will read what we've written and hear the pitch, tone, even the question, as Penelope Fitzgerald says, that we might not yet hear ourselves asking.

∾

In Fitzgerald's book *The Blue Flower,* an eighteenth-century portrait artist named Hoffman has been hired to paint the brilliant protagonist's beloved, a thirteen-year-old country girl, decent and kind in every way. Hoffman spends days with Sophie at her parents' home, thinking, he says, behind the closed door of his top-floor room. At the end of a week, he packs up his supplies and leaves, having completed only a few spare sketches. Hoping to avoid his patron, Hoffman travels to a nearby town and holes up in a pub where his patron arrives and buys him a beer.

What happened to the portrait? the patron wants to know. Do you need more time?

Hoffman's explanation has haunted me for years: It's not about time, he tries to explain. I wait to hear, he insists, that inaudible query I believe is at the center of every single life. "I could not hear her question," he laments, "and so I could not paint."

∾

On my mother's windowsill the next morning, the bottle reflects the light, casts a green shimmer on the nearby table. Inside, blurred writing on the note is clearly visible. She wants me to leave it there, says maybe she'll paint it next week.

I'm aware that my father, worried about the danger to bare feet in the sand or to a boat's propeller, would have thrown it in the trash. Pragmatic, safety conscious, he'd have had no interest in the light glass can cast or the way a washed-up bottle with a note makes me muse about a perfect listener. Hard work, he'd say, gets us places. If he were Daedalus, he'd have found something other than wings to free us from the maze. *Read the charts,* he'd remind me out on the bay, *and steer clear of shoals. You'll be fine.*

How to tell him I wanted to be more than fine? That I wanted for myself the kind of mind that could come up with a line like Auden's or Fitzgerald's. It's what I imagined my mother once wanted, too. She probably couldn't explain it to him either: *Parents with a Green Bottle between Them Talk in Different Languages.* Could I ever ask her about that?

She's standing at the window, inching the bottle sideways on the sill.

Will you look for jingle shells on the beach today? she asks.

I, too, would like to see them in this light at the bottle's base. Maybe something coarse, as well — a piece of scrap metal bent at right angles. For the left side, almost touching the glass.

Will you? she asks again.

I've known for a long time she sees the world aesthetically — for lack of a better word — but I've never heard her talk like this or muse about objects she might someday paint. And then more: she tells me about a washed-up bottle she found once on the beach where I'd been walking the day before. Inside, on a damp piece of paper, blurred words. She could make out only a few letters: *perdid* . . . Or *pesa* . . ? Loss? Grief? Though she didn't know the language — Spanish, she guessed — she believed she knew the feeling behind it. In fact, she claims, she didn't want to know the details. "The best way to hear Mass is when you don't know the language," Auden says — another line of his that occurs to me now.

Sure it was never meant to be found, she recorked the bottle, but then couldn't decide what to do with it. If she dropped it off the end of a pier, she tells me, it'd just wash ashore again. Someone else would pick it up, maybe drop it in the trash.

I buried it, she finally says. *Under a bush by the back door of that place on Bay Street where I used to live.*

If there's a question at the center of my mother's life, I don't know what it is.

What note would you put in a bottle? I finally ask her.

You first, she counters.

There it is, I think. Neither of us has a clue. Perhaps we should have listened harder.

Or else Fitzgerald is wrong. Do any of us, after all, really want a single question to compel our lives? Or a caption to substitute for an array of feelings? She brushes off a few grains of sand and moves the bottle two inches into shadow. Half the glass darkens from chartreuse to olive.

There, she says, backing out of the way. Then, what I imagine but don't hear her say: Do you see now what your father couldn't see?

And I do, though I don't mention that either. Instead, I listen to this unexpected chord we've seldom struck and study the way the window frames her silver hair, her ivory bathrobe, her hands about to drop to her sides. Outside the window, nothing falling. Just the cloudless Florida sky.

11 BEACHED ICEBERGS
Erasable Truths

> We go wrong mostly
> by insisting the world is rimmed
> with un-erasable truths.
> — KATHLEEN GRABER

1

I admit I went immediately to the indentation in black sand. Big enough to step into, turn around in. Grizzly bed? Former site of a camper's tent? I'm drawn to the evidence of disappearance. I like, as many of us do, the mystery a vacancy suggests. Something was here, something left, and just below the high-tide line a single clue remains.

No yeti paw print, no sign of moose hoof. The only footprints here on the Alaskan shore are mine. There's no sign of anything walking or crawling away from this indentation, no scraped troughs in the sand, no litter of debris trailing away from where I stand in the middle. No exit sign at all.

The only hint: inside the circle, the black sand is darker, wetter. If I didn't know better, I'd crane my neck, double-check that nothing between it and the sun is casting a shadow on the cinders.

2

Glaciologists call them wallow depressions. How can I not think about bogged-down-in-sadness? Every bluesy note densing into more blue and then black, the pitiful pleasure we get from nuzzling our own woe.

The only thing that erases them, they say, are more of what brings them in: the tide at full strength, the wind behind it, storms.

3

Just north along the beach two more wallows and further yet, what causes them: an iceberg beached by high tide. No messy wrack line today, just this pristine figurine that squats in the sand, as if delivered there from Tiffany's and recently unwrapped.

Chunks of fresh water calved from glaciers up north, some icebergs are deep blue and gritty like the stuff I used to scrape from defrosting fridges, coarse, pebbly, nothing I'd want in my mouth. This one is whiter, the result of air bubbles trapped inside. It would have floated like something majestic down the bay, its gazillion crystals reflecting the light, its pinnacles like bright steeples.

4

Whoever thinks icebergs keep drifting serenely hasn't watched them for long. At some point, they list, turn on their sides, roll over. Pinnacles melt, shifting the weight; crevasses widen; bases worn by sloshing seawater shrink; the berg goes belly-up.

5

The tide and the wind swept this one ashore, lowered it here, and retreated. I wish I could say it's still beautiful. True, its sharp edges have been softened by warmth, but it's lost whatever dignity sculpted ice can have. As it melts, trapped air escapes; crystals squeak, water drips, the berg begins to groan. It seems tired, finished, a diminished thing. It can do nothing now but grow smaller. It will never move again. As the day wears on it looks more and more like a shrinking piece of Styrofoam against the backdrop of Alaskan wilderness. So much of what seems solid — I might be talking about the beliefs of my youth — does nothing more than this berg does: ends up stranded in a place it can't survive. Around it, the stain spreads, the sand darkens.

6

I remember when I believed hermits had the best chance of knowing who they are and, as much as I could, arranged my life like that, lots of solitude and introspection. It was easy to let that tendency harden into a truth when the climate all around was cool, the view uninterrupted. And when I fell in love and discovered just the opposite, truths like that just disappeared, evaporated.

"From the place where we are right / flowers will never grow," the poet Yehuda Amichai says. Uncertainty's more fertile ground, but living there is tough. The truth is, when I stand in this warming wallow, I can still feel the damp aftermath, what's left when a berg's own weight and the sun have pressed it into sand, made it a ghost with an imposing footprint.

12 WORMS

The Persistence of Habits

Habits are cobwebs at first; cables at last.

— CHINESE PROVERB

SOMETIMES THE BEACH SEEMS too damp and soft for the spare kind of thinking I'm trying to do these days. Too full of forgiveness, too yielding. Wouldn't Vesuvius be a better site to study the rough edges and frictions against which our sensibilities are honed? Our response to catastrophe, I've often thought, is more revealing than our habits, though now I'm not so sure.

Meanwhile, I'm back on Cape Ann, Massachusetts, where the rocks are submerged and then bared, and the seaweed lies parched and then drenched. On the north end of the beach, three painters squint at the hull of a wrecked fishing boat that twice daily disappears and reappears at the edge of the harbor. Further out, a white sail grows smaller. Looking east out over the ocean, I remember reading once about a worm, *Convoluta roscoffensis,* which streaks the sands of Normandy with green. At first glance, the description suggests, you think of algae smears or some delicate seaweed strewn in slathers. But if you watched from above the high-tide line, you'd notice that the receding tide doesn't deposit the green stuff, that, in fact, it seems to emerge from under the sand once the water has withdrawn. And if you approached, leaned down, and looked closely, you'd see that the green swaths are not gunks of algae or seaweed at all but millions of tiny, spinach-colored flat-worms that have wriggled up from under the sand to sunbathe between tides. Twice a day they squirm to the surface to bask, and they never mistime their emergence, never rise too soon or too late into a surf that would drown them in an instant.

The worms themselves don't need the sun, but the creatures inside them do, and they keep the worm alive. Symbiosis, scientists call it. In this case, the process begins before the worm is hatched and a certain kind of algae — *Tetraselmis* — burrows inside a flatworm's egg. Once hatched, the juvenile worm with its algae inside feeds like most worms do, swallowing plankton and bacteria. But by the time it's an adult and host to twenty-five thousand of those small, plantlike creatures, there's no need for mouth or pharynx, which atrophy and disappear. There's no need to feed at all, for the algae's photosynthesis produces sugars and starches, which the worm absorbs for nutrition.

Imagine bringing something into your body and agreeing to feed off one another for the rest of your lives — no backing out, no rethinking the commitment. The worm requires nothing of the algae except that it live inside it; the algae requires nothing of the worm except that it shelter it and, crucially, that it sunbathe twice a day. The worm obliges, and, with millions of others, unburies itself during every daytime low tide, soaks up enough sun for its algae to turn light into food. When the tide turns, the worm must avoid drowning or being washed out to sea and so sinks again into the sand.

In the human realm, such symbiosis — vital and incontrovertible — makes me wary. I like my time alone too much to be so bound to another. Or is that particular psychology simply my habit?

Here's what's even more compelling, perhaps more familiar too: When scientists moved a small colony of the worms to the bottom of a tideless aquarium in a lab, the worms — even without the tide — continued to emerge twice daily from the sandy bottom. They have no brain to speak of, nothing we'd call memory or habit, yet still they rose up and sank back in some ancient rhythm, as if the tide itself flooded and ebbed inside their flat and puny bodies.

I don't like to think of myself as similarly governed, though I assume most of us at least partially, maybe secretly, are. And though catastrophe might make us more visible to others, I suspect now it's our habits — useful, neurotic, mindless, comforting — that can, if we're willing, teach us about ourselves. Like well-worn grooves in the psyche, they become who we are and have more to do with our temperaments than does high drama or heroic action. Tomorrow the artists will do what they do with their brushes and paint; sailors will study the wind. I'll return to this beach and walk in soft sand, try again to behave — how can I help it? — as if I might someday know what any of this means.

13 JELLYFISH
The Unfinished

There is nothing final about a mistake,
except its being taken as final.
— PHYLLIS BOTTOME

I SHOULD HAVE KNOWN that at some point on these beach excursions I'd come across a jellyfish. They're everywhere in the Chesapeake Bay this time of year, drifting north, trailing filmy tentacles and annoying swimmers with their toxins. Sometimes currents and tides bring them too close to shore, leave them baking in the sand. Now this one — a sea nettle — lies splat at my feet, milky white and paled to the point of translucence.

I prod it with my boot; it dimples but doesn't break open or spurt. I don't know if it's dead or alive, repulsive or beautiful. Mostly, it looks like a mistake, the kind I've seen on the floor of a glassblower's studio after the artist gathered hot glass from the furnace, twirled it around his blowpipe, and then dropped it. He wouldn't confuse that blunder with a finished piece. Nor would he bother to complete its careful hardening process, which is what this thing at my feet looks as if it needs.

It's been years since I spent summers in the bay with my father, swimming and dodging jelly flotilla, dabbing meat tenderizer or baby powder on stings I couldn't avoid. Walking the wrack line by the blue-gray waters in which his ashes now drift, I've been thinking a lot lately about how the word *finished* can have such opposite connotations. If a ballerina is finished, her career is over, but when a soufflé is finished, it's perfect. Finishing schools smack of superficiality, but finishing touches imply elegant, subtle completions. When wood is finished, its beauty deepens; when a rose is finished, it begins to stink. If a mission is finished, it's either completed or ruined.

Seemingly stuck somewhere between beginning and end, jellyfish look *un*finished, like some kind of neonatal oddity, a just-delivered rudimentary mass in the incubatory warmth of the sand. This one resembles an embryo that ran out of time to develop shell or scales or a covering of any kind to keep the interior intact. Its transparency, too, suggests prematurity, as if it hadn't had time to perfect concealment, protect what's inside. I can look right into it and see that it has no bones or brain, not even a heart. What little interior work has been completed is still visible — what I think are gonads and the white lines of canals that transport food.

Jellies don't look ruined either. Despite the appearance of incompletion, out in the water they're paragons of grace in a body that seems almost erased, every motion fluid, undulant, without the possibility of fidget or fall. Otherworldly beautiful, swaying water-ghosts with names equally evocative: moons and lion's manes, mushroom caps and crown jellies, cradles and jellied bougainvillea.

And if ruined means unsuccessful, I can't say the jelly is that either. In fact, they're an evolutionary success — 670 million years old, older than dinosaurs — and still thriving. Even the mountains where I live — uplifted and eroded, drowned, and uplifted again, now old and worn — aren't that old or stable. While those peaks have grown soft and rounded and the valleys broad, the jellies have changed very little. They've found the formula for survival and are in no danger of extinction. Yet for all its success and beauty, this one at my feet repels.

In marine field guides, the diagrams of jellyfish are often drawn with delicate white lines and streams of white points on glossy black pages. They look like a biologist's version of unfinished connect-the-dots games, their outlines as tentative as their insides. Or like constellations, but without fixed points or celestial positions. The guidebooks say the distribution of many jellies is unknown. Some never wash ashore, some live in the deep, one species evidently surfaces only at night. They pulse by contracting muscles beneath the bell, forcing water out. With each slow-motion expulsion, they glide backward. When they relax those muscles, the bell opens; the jellies pause, drifting in their own underwater galaxies, almost invisible, in a world that seems totally apart from ours.

Except when they sting. In July, they infest the bay with their diaphanous moons and poisonous tentacles, on which the human body seems to exert a gravitational pull. It doesn't matter if the water's clear when you first enter it or, years ago, that my siblings and I used to take turns acting as sentry on the stern of my father's boat, one of us scanning the water as the others dove and swam. Within ten minutes they seemed to start closing in, more than a constellation, a whole galaxy collecting itself, beginning to swirl around their center, which happened to be one of us in a bathing suit with plenty of flesh exposed. It felt like attack and we, otherwise indomitable teenagers, would squeal and scramble for the ladder, hoisting our feet up as high and fast as we could while the filmy creatures drifted by, just below us. The truth is sea nettles aren't aggressive and they don't prey on humans. They're eyeless and can see nothing of us. We swim by them and a tentacle brushes across our calves and a hundred nematocysts fire simultaneously. Nothing personal, nothing fatal, a mere itch and sting. To be stung is simply a sign of unintended contact.

Not all jellyfish are so benign. The most deadly marine animal in the entire world — deadlier than great white sharks — is a pale-blue jelly that'll kill a human in less than five minutes. Almost invisible, it swims off the coast of Australia, dragging its ten-foot-long tentacles, each of them armed with up to five thousand nematocysts. A sting causes almost instant excruciating pain, followed immediately by shock and respiratory arrest and near-certain death. Unlike the nettles of my childhood, that one — called a box jelly — has eyes. Four of them. No one knows how they process the information the eyes receive, but the creature can avoid objects in the water, change directions, turn corners to prevent collisions. And unlike the sea nettle, box jellies are strong swimmers. They can resist current, aim for shore during an ebb tide, and propel themselves, some say, as fast as seven feet a second.

Tentacles pull its prey, a shrimp, say, into its square bell, at the center of which is the manubrium, a tubelike structure that extends itself to and then around the shrimp and then engulfs it. Imagine lips that can hover above a table and grow long enough to dangle over the entrée, which they then pluck from the plate. Within a minute, the shrimp has disappeared into the bell, its nutrients dispersed along radial canals to all parts of what passes for a body. The fact that the manubrium acts as both mouth and anus doesn't help my sense of its incompletion. Wasn't there time to develop separate structures? It seems that another week or two of development would result in something that makes more engineering sense.

∾

Never begin what you can't finish, my father once insisted. I was ten; we were standing over an outdoor rabbit pen I was trying to fashion out of chicken wire. Stumped by my inability to make the cage escape-proof, I nodded my head. But if he were alive now I'd want to ask him how can I ever tell what's finishable, what's not? How can I always know at the outset that this is something I can bring to completion or will have to give up on, discard in midform? Even as an adult, I'm drawn to so many things I might never complete — writing a novel, playing a Bach partita, planting a garden of constant white blooms. And though I tend to keep my false starts and failed attempts private, I'm aware that to never begin such things would likely cause more angst than to leave them half undone.

I think of Franz Schubert, who never finished his B minor symphony. Nobody knows why. Theories abound — syphilis stopped him, or depression or Beethoven's triumphs — but the mystery has remained for more than a hundred years. He didn't even acknowledge that he'd begun an eighth symphony, and it wasn't until thirty years after his death that someone found it. Did he not want to admit to an abandoned project? Why didn't he throw it away instead of handing it to someone whose brother stuffed it in the back of a drawer? For years I wondered if it haunted him, if he still worked secretly at his piano on the third movement, hoping he could take the clarinet solo and moments of stillness near the end of the second and explode them into a triumphant finish.

When people listen to Schubert's *Unfinished Symphony* do they feel, as I do when I look at this jellyfish, that it seems unfinished? Unsatisfying? That's not my reaction to the music, and here's why: what starts out as dialogue between hope and despair shape-shifts in the second movement from drama to poem. The first movement reminds us of how we long for resolution; the second movement reminds us how to live without it. When it's over and the sound of those last strings dies down, I'm aware that something I can't imagine doesn't happen next. It's a delicious, irresolvable anticipation, and Schubert allows it to linger forever.

But because a jellyfish is a physical object that looks so blatantly unfinished, I begin to fill in the gaps, imagine a shell, scales, some kind of fins. What it lacks seems tangible and makes what is there unsatisfying.

∾

In Latin, *re infecta* means "the matter being unfinished." The term is used to describe incomplete plans: "We part, *re infecta*," Robert Louis Stevenson notes, referring to unresolved tax matters. "Mr. Rose's mission is terminated *re infecta*," writes Thomas Jefferson to Levi Lincoln. I think of the term, however, not evaluatively, but philosophically. What matters — our values, our imaginations — are not set in stone. They can shift and deepen or evaporate. Same with matter itself, meaning substance, material, sand, clay, wood, glass. All of it changes constantly, erodes, disintegrates, transforms into something else. The term doesn't suggest to me incompletion of a completable mission or a pending decision. It suggests a chronic condition, an ongoing state of affairs in which things are constantly evolving or devolving, metamorphosing.

Every culture recognizes transformation. We see it in the hundreds of myths of shape-shifting: Daphne gets changed into a laurel tree, Castor and Pollux into stars, frogs into princes, human bowels into jellyfish. Such is the origin, according to Maori legend, of these gelatinous sacs. Ruatapu, son of a Maori king, seeking revenge for an insult, sank a boatload of children and was drowned by the gods as punishment. His bowels, loosed from his bloated body, grew round and tentacled and pulsed rhythmically away in the Tasman Sea.

From the Japanese, a different story: A swimming creature with bones and fins and feet was sent by a dragon king to fetch a live monkey's liver. When it botched the mission, the dragon king beat the bones out of the creature, pulverized its feet and fins, reduced it to a pulp, and flung it back into the sea.

We think in terms of evolution more often than mythology these days, but even evolution suggests that change — incremental, accidental, adaptive — teems everywhere. Fish clamber ashore and grow legs, humans begin to walk upright, bacteria mutate to avoid antibiotics. There's no end in sight to this perpetual flux, this world *re infecta*.

With my boot, I roll the jellyfish again, watch it blubber over and re-splat itself in the sand. Six inches across, dozens of tentacles, some of them three feet long. Useless now, they lie tangled and sandy. Unlike a fish or penguin, which can at least flop or waddle on shore, a jellyfish on land is utterly stranded. It has no way of crawling or rolling toward the tide, back into the sea. Out there, its movement is primitive, but in here, without water, it can't move at all.

And without a penis or vagina, neither can it copulate: there's nothing to put and no place to put it. Sexual reproduction means releasing eggs (often as many as forty thousand a day) and sperm (millions) into the sea where their drift and collision might result in a planula, a microscopic, swimming larva that eventually attaches itself to an underwater surface and metamorphoses into a polyp. When biologists first discovered polyps on the bottom of the sea, they classified them as plants. Fixed to the ocean floor, they resemble tiny fleshy trees waving their branchlike bulbous tentacles — it's a mistake that'd be easy to make. No wonder biologists hunted for spores and ignored the tiny creatures floating nearby as something unrelated. It wasn't until the eighteenth century that they realized the polyps nourished themselves not through photosynthesis but with the microscopic creatures they swept into their mouths.

Polyps reproduce asexually: they grow buds, which become more polyps, which grow more buds and polyps, which eventually become a small colony. At some point, the colony releases free-swimming medusas, which are the bells we see pulsing around in salt or brackish water. The medusa is a voracious feeder and grows fast. Its tentacles, which stun its prey — comb jellies and tiny crustaceans, minnows, worms, and mosquito larvae — and herd them into the mouth, can work independently of each other. Picture an active teenager with four dozen ghostly hands cruising up and down a loaded buffet table.

Though lots of food, ideal salinity, and few predators mean high probability of survival, a medusa seldom lives more than a few months. By October, most of them are dead. But under the bay, attached to the bottom, to seaweed and oyster shells, millions of polyps lie dormant until the water warms again in spring and their plantlike bodies begin to swell and bud, releasing thousands more tiny medusas into the water where they drift and swim and sting for yet another season.

$\sim$

Sometimes when I'm listening to a Bach or Schubert symphony, I think if I could play like that, I'd never want to do anything else. Naive, I know, even as I know that such longings keep me from feeling I'm finished with dreams. Of all the things I've pined for over the years, I've let go of several and held on to a few. None of this makes me fret or despair. In fact, I'm fond of my longings; they're part of who I am as much as the scar on my leg and the curve in my spine. I like the reminder of improbable possibilities, the challenge of living well when something's forever incomplete. And isn't this, finally, the way of the world?

What seems done one day — a garden design, an argument, a repair job on a sagging step — shows signs of change the next. Forget-me-nots invade the iris bed, the sullenness persists, the nail's popped up again. And after so many things in my life — marriage, parents, notions of self — radically changed, I'm learning, maybe too adamantly, to never quite yield to any declaration of "finished," to not put much stock in stasis. What business of importance, after all, is ever fully completed? I don't mean the obvious: projects, buildings, events on a calendar. I mean the things that we might say have to do with the soul, whose business is to stay unsettled.

And that, I see now, is why the jellyfish disturbs me: I fret about flagrant displays of incompletion, the likelihood that longings too soon exposed will wither or turn grotesque. For me, those unsettled stirrings need a bit of quiet, a chance to churn in the private dark. The jelly, of course, has no sense of soul or uncompleted business, but we humans ought to, and so, for instance, when a student brandishes to the class a just-written poem, its lines all akimbo, no flesh on its bones, I want him to return it to his notebook, worry it along for a while in secret sessions with himself. Few mistakes are final, but for many of them a little cloistered toil might hurry along a revision.

The tide reminds me today not that any mistake can be rectified but that it's likely to be repeated, and too often in full public view. I know that perfection is rare and completion a goal most of us won't reach. The glassblower will drop his dollop onto the floor, the musician will hit a wrong note, jellyfish will wash ashore again, looking each time like embryos with their edges tattered and gnawed. We'll fail once more; we'll be unkind, give up too soon, blame someone else, deny we have dreams we'll never fulfill. Mostly, the world goes on, *re infecta.* We ourselves go on, *re infecta.* Couldn't greater cognizance of this inspire a bit of discretion, a thoughtful hesitance before pronouncements?

I jab the jellyfish with a stick, lightly. I can see its insides jiggle, its food canals twitch. How resilient its shimmer is, how firm its borders. Jellyfish are tough. I've seen young kids stomp on them, and they lie in the sand intact. Is this one finished? I still don't know if it's dead or alive, but I do know this: even after death, the jelly's nematocysts lie coiled and full of toxin. If I touch it, it can still shoot venom into my hand.

14 PEBBLES

Fine Distinctions

> The uncanny is not some new thing but a thing known
> returning in a different form, become a revenant.
> — JOHN BANVILLE

THOUGH THE MERMAN HAS NOTHING to do with my original reason for visiting Orford Ness, his story has complicated my musings about stones and shingle beaches. Local fishermen claimed they had caught him in their nets, a slithery creature, man from the waist up, fish from the waist down. They grabbed him under his arms and dragged him across the shingle beach, his tail flopping and flailing over the pebbles, which must have rolled and shifted a bit in his wake, darkened by seawater shaken from his scales. The villagers feared him. They took him to the bottom of the castle keep, bound him up in the dark, beat him, and finally, in a last resort to get him to speak, they hung him by his tail over a fire. *Burn,* they tried to get him to say. *Scare.*

The English warden who'd dropped me at the edge of the Orford Ness Nature Reserve on the southwest coast of Suffolk wanted to know what my interest was, why I'd searched out this place now closed to tourists. I didn't say anything about the merman, whom I'd first heard of just last night at a local art gallery when a woman who knew of my planned trip to the ness had approached me, her eyes glittering. Nor did I say I'd been intrigued by the various descriptions of the ness that I'd run across in my reading: "aura of mystique," "wild and hostile," "potentially dangerous."

Debris, I told the warden, especially debris that's washed up by the sea — kelp, bottles, driftwood, stone. And shore regions formed by debris — coastal moraines and shingle beaches. He'd been understandably reluctant at first, but finally agreed to take me by boat and then by jeep out to this barren spit that juts into the North Sea. His only caution: stay off the shingle above the high-water mark. *If you're not back at the landing jetty in a few hours,* he said as he turned the jeep around, *I'll come back out and look for you.*

Last night in my hotel room after the gallery opening, I unwrapped a package the glittery-eyed woman had delivered to me — a musty book published in 1700 — and turned the yellowed pages carefully to the marked passage about the Merman of Orford. There the historian recounts the tale told by a monkish chronicler about a creature caught in the fishing nets off of what became, centuries later, the shingle beach at Orford. Half man, half fish, bearded and scaly, the story says, a wild man who fought the nets that tangled him and the men who locked him up in the dungeon of a nearby castle. The woman from the art gallery evidently believed in a literal merman. I think she wanted me to also.

On the beach this drizzly November morning, the castle keep and its dungeon behind me, I picture the fishermen on the sea, eyeing the wind, hauling nets, calculating the odds of a good catch just a few miles farther out, where survival depends on knowing what the water holds. They catch sight of something they can't identify, something that lures, as the strange often does, a vision or a fear that requires an explanation. A sea turtle with tendrils? A squid with expression? What to think of a creature who resembles you but lives in a way that you cannot? Did they fear the merman, finally, because he was too much like them or not enough? They did what we humans too often do: imagined what might scare them and then created that very thing so they could drag it ashore, tie it up in a castle, make it feel what they didn't want to: *burn, scare.*

The warden has driven off. To both sides and in front of me, a desert of pebbles extends almost as far as I can see, a vast mosaic of flindered ochre and gray. No honking horns, cell phones, the sound of anything human. Out here on the ness, no trees provide shelter, no butte or peak breaks up the terrain. Just acres of tiny stones underfoot and a silence that's almost eerie. Even the sea is quiet. Unfolding old and current maps, I try to figure out exactly where they hauled the merman ashore and realize the beach I'm standing on wasn't even here a thousand years ago. On a 1601 map, the earliest one I have, the ness, which means nose, is north of the town of Orford and extends farther up and out into the water, as if sniffing the North Sea a little snootily. Five hundred years earlier, when the merman came ashore, it would have been even farther north, somewhere up near my hotel in Aldeburgh.

So, I asked the woman last night in the gallery, *was he fish or human? Both,* she insisted. But how? How did he get that way? Human sex with a fish is preposterous, as is the notion of either of them giving birth to the result. *No,* she said, *not like that. He just came into being. Appeared.* This is the stuff I'm drawn to, these stories of transformation: Kwakiutl lore about salmon turning into twins, Inuit stories of bears into men, quick-change artists like Spider-Man, Superman, Wonder Woman.

I like to imagine a slow-motion camera recording the change — scales thinning into skin, fur dropping out, fingers growing webby — and wonder whether we're ever aware of the drifts and shifts of our own lives, the moments when we find ourselves, through tragedy or good fortune, a slightly altered being, sprouting new strengths, new skills or vices, becoming more or less than we were. Is there ever a morning when we look in the mirror and suspect we're seeing a different face?

No, she insisted, it just appeared.

Today the ness is about ten miles long, a shifting pile of the debris of ancient landforms. It's made up, almost exclusively, of pebbles, the polished, transported bits of more-northerly lands. Technically, *shingle* refers to sediment smaller than boulders but larger than sand or, more specifically, stones with a diameter between two and two hundred millimeters. Somewhere up the coast of England there must have been, millions of years ago, ledges and mountains of granite and flint, maybe chert and quartzite that got hammered and battered by rain and the sea. Small chunks would have been broken off by waves that tumbled them for centuries, lifting and rolling, scouring and polishing, moving them southward in the direction of prevailing storms, piling them up along the coast in low ridges. Where the shoreline tucks a little inland, as it does just south of Orford, the storms decrease and the effect is even more dramatic: winds die down, the wave action slows, and the water, unable to keep moving its load of pebbles, drops it. The noselike beach accumulates another layer there, grows a little deeper and longer. Today there's not a jagged stone in sight, no hooks or pocks or anything rough. Just globes and oblongs, glassy ovals and orbs, smooth-sided, sometimes perfect Os. Tiny petrified eggs.

Most shingle beaches are barren. Rain splashes against the pebbles and drops immediately into tiny interstices, millions of rivulets vanishing into the spaces between stones. There's nothing to slow the water, no tiny pit whose bottom doesn't lead to passageways farther below. Whenever it rains, these millions of pebbles are merely rinsed, never drenched. And it isn't just the lack of moisture that discourages plant life. These same glassy-smooth stones that shrug off water also refuse the dirt. This beach is the cleanest expanse of stones I've ever seen.

And, it seems, the most raked. Even from the ground where I'm standing, I can see the pattern of ridges and valleys running mostly parallel to the shoreline. The larger pebbles congregate in the valleys and the lighter ones, called *fines,* pile up in mostly parallel ridges just a few feet away. The valleys are a hue darker; the ridges are lighter, more sand-colored, and delicate. The result is a subtle striping that changes slightly if I look across rather than lengthwise along the ridges. It changes again when the fog lightens and clouds thin, as if this were a beach of wide-wale corduroy and someone's fingers were alternately smoothing and roughing up the nap.

That's an illusion, of course, the kind that provides a moment's pleasure without the risk of hardening into dogma about the hand of any god or which way one should stand if the sun is shining or not. In actuality, stone-sorting here is the result of the waves' depositing the stones in a series of ridges and swales sculpted only by certain laws of physics — wave action and lift, pebble weight and deposition.

Most of us humans, on the other hand, sort with a certain degree of consciousness. It seems to be one of our traits to like things assigned to specific categories. Classifying is one of the first tasks of discrimination a young child learns: all the red objects belong in this pile, blue in another. Squares over here and circles over there.

When I was twelve or thirteen and spending summer days on the beaches of the Atlantic Ocean, I used to try to classify seashells. With my bare foot, I'd draw around me four or five large circles in the sand, and then I'd stand with my bucket of shells like a kid at the start of a hopscotch game, tossing the fan-shaped shells into one circle, horns into another, turkey wings there, cones into the circle beside me. I didn't know the language of bivalves or gastropods, and function didn't matter. Shape did. When I found a shell that didn't fit any of my categories — too twisted or barnacled, too odd to be typed — I heaved it back into the water. Only a few merited their own miscellaneous category — ones with deep purplish color or an inside curve so lustrous I'd keep my thumb in it half the afternoon. Beauty, I see now, could break the rules, but the grotesque could not. I don't remember making up stories about the shells, the way I did with stones in the backyard. Looking back, it seemed to be merely an exercise in the pleasure of sorting, perhaps a human tendency to group: golf balls in one pile, baseballs in another, scholars in one place, athletes in another. Large stones in the valleys, smaller ones on the ridges, humans in one category, fish in another.

For us, there's safety and efficiency to such clear categories, and often laziness. For the English sea pea, however, there's an imperative. Size-sorted stone is crucial, in fact, if the shingle is to support any plant life at all. Here's why: a larger stone has more rounded surface area than a small one and therefore can't nestle as closely to surrounding, also rounded, stones. As a result, there are larger spaces between the larger rocks, which means more space for rain and dirt to slip through. Picture pouring dirt through a clutch of ping-pong balls. The interstices gape, so that that which might support plant life slips through the holes and disappears.

Or, the holes in the mind-sieve widen too far, so that inhibitions drop away. Rationality can find no foothold. Nor can a tolerance for ambiguity or thoughtfulness about fantasies. And that which might ordinarily be repressed slips out too soon, appears only half-transformed: a merman, a centaur. Is this what can happen out at sea or wherever fear combines with lack of bearings? Subtleties vanish; the world becomes starker and the mind more coarse.

But on the ridges here, where the pebbles are smaller, they can nestle together more closely, like lima beans or even lentils. The spaces between them are tighter, which is what the sea pea needs. Though it has a long taproot to snake and curl through the shingle, the rare plant depends on bits of organic debris and the drop or two of moisture that only a congregation of smaller stones can trap. Records indicate that the sea pea was once abundant on the shingle in the mid-1500s, a few hundred years after the merman, when it was harvested by villagers in Aldeburgh during a famine. It isn't plentiful now. In fact, that it grows here at all makes the beach a designated Site of Special Scientific Interest. The story of its near extinction in this area is a story about secret radar and war and the triggering devices on atomic bombs.

Bouncing over the shingle in his jeep, the warden had told me part of the history. In the late 1960s, he said, when the American Armed Forces were hunting for a site on which to build the world's largest, most sophisticated, most powerful radar of its kind, they chose the shingle beach of Orford Ness. Isolated, quiet, uninhabited, the Ness provided the secrecy the military needed, a spot where, they calculated, reception would be unimpeded and the project could operate under a cloak of mystery. Cobra Mist consisted of a giant, fan-shaped array of aerials arranged in a 119-degree arc and, with its large aluminum ground net, covering over eighty acres. The aerials themselves ranged from forty to almost two hundred feet high. Costing more than one hundred million dollars, the project never worked. Its ability to receive signals was, from the start, hampered by the presence of a mysterious noise. "Clutter-related noise," they called it. "Severe background noise," "excessive noise of undetermined origin." Months of testing failed to find the source of the problem.

UFOs again, a local contingent muttered. Though the warden hadn't mentioned this, I learned from others that Orford Ness has long been a hotbed of spaceship stories, accounts of fireballs and strange lights, hovering, cigar-shaped aircraft. Perhaps, some hypothesized, UFO residue interfered with the radar's function. Maybe there were even UFOs still using the ness as a landing site. More tests, more theories. In the end, the armed forces admitted they couldn't explain the interference and dismantled the huge array. But the damage to Orford Ness had been done — roads built, wells dug, and barracks erected, all of which meant boots, tires, and shovels in the shingle. Intent on cupping a huge ear to the sky, they shuffled the pebbles until the fines were mixed into the coarser, the distinction disappeared, dirt and rain slipped through the cracks, and most of the sea peas died.

In 2000, the National Trust tried reconstructing the shingle, using sieves and screens to re-sort the pebbles, move the small ones back to the ridges, the larger ones to the valleys. They measured the height and width of nearby undamaged ridges and swales and constructed the newly re-sorted mounds accordingly. On some of the new ridges, they experimented with adding extremely fine pebbles and on others, seeds, sometimes both. Using fixed-point photography, they monitored any plant growth. But months later, it all seemed futile. The rate of plant colonization did not increase, and the labor-intensive nature of the work made the whole experiment too costly. The trust concluded that no amount of human effort can replicate what the tides and the waves do naturally.

Restoring the sea pea and the shingle beach wasn't at all what Derek Jarman had in mind. Thirty-seven miles south of Orford on the shingle beach at Dungeness, the artist, dying of AIDS, moved rocks and pebbles, built basins with plastic liners, hauled in manure, fashioned a garden on the barren shingle. He raked the gravel into furrows and circles, upended larger stones, piled up pebbles of blue-gray that he ringed with flat flint, and collected debris from the beach. Around his cottage, sculptures of twisted iron scraps rise out of mounds of gorse and elder. Everywhere there's a sense of the deliberate — stones balanced on upright driftwood, a scavenged orange glove cradling a yellow pebble in its palm. Poppies bloom along with viper's bugloss, pink valerian, and giant sea kale. "Paradise," he decided not long before he died.

Unlike the villagers inclined to torment fish-tailed men or the waves governed only by the laws of physics, Jarman did his work consciously and slowly. For eight years he walked and collected, dug and raked, planted and rearranged, stood back and reconsidered. That's the difference between a myth like the merman or the inattentiveness of the army and the work of an artist. Jarman took forms and rearranged them. He had an aesthetic in mind. What emerged in his garden wasn't by sudden metamorphosis — the shingle blooming into lushness overnight — but by the long slow business of beauty: worry, watering, the slow coaxing of an oasis of color and shape.

I turn and head north. Walking, even meditative walking, isn't easy. *Arduous*, in fact, the warden had warned me. The pebbles can roll, give way underfoot, leave your ankle turned sideways. You can't predict if they'll stay still enough to give the ball of your foot something firm to push off of or if you'll stumble forward, lurch a little, leave a small stone-slide in your wake. With my foot, I could rake them — clean and rounded — into small ridges, much like Japanese monks have done with gravel and sand for centuries. Their gardens are serene and silent, just the conditions for opening the mind. I bend down and pick up a handful, let them dribble into mounds at my knees, small collapsing piles of pebbles — copper colored, adobe, gray speckled and plum, small nuggets with streaks of black. The pile builds until it can't keep itself together. Pebbles roll down its side, a pyramid of slowly avalanching, giant grains of sand.

I've done this hundreds of times on the beaches of my childhood, mounding the damp and silent sand with my feet, dropping to my knees to pat it into grainy sculptures. But shingle pebbles aren't silent; they ping and clatter and clunk. They don't cling to one another, hold any shape at all. Castles and forts are as impossible, finally, as the fantasy of a miniature me in a colossal garden of Zen. No monk raked the small stones, no hooded contemplative strolls silently by or sits cross-legged, trying to empty the mind. No tool is old or large enough to be the vast rake that the North Sea is, heaping and sorting the shingle for centuries. And no Zen garden I've ever heard of posts signs like the one to my left: "Danger. Unexploded Ordnance. Please Keep to Visitor Route."

To the south I can barely make out the outline of two Japanese-looking pagodas. The rooflines — gracefully curved — are consistent with the Zen-like feel of the place. Built fifty years ago, they were designed to shelter, not monks, but the triggers for atomic bombs. Below the roof was a pit into which the trigger mechanism of a bomb could be gently lowered. After it had been carefully placed and vibration sensors attached, the pit was sealed, and the tests begun. They subjected the triggering device to various vibrations, temperature shocks, and a hydraulic ram that could produce *g*-forces. If the thing detonated, the roof, a light aluminum, would be blown off harmlessly.

I try to imagine the tests — the device buried in the well, the beach pebbled and still all around it and then the vibrations and ramming, the temperature shocks, the shingle pounded, the small stones rattling, the trigger down in its well absorbing one blast after another after another until finally it's too much and the bomb explodes, blows off the aluminum roof. Surely the mind does likewise. Surely there's a point where what's been under the surface can absorb no more and erupts in passion or fear, fantasies and hallucinations. With no time or consciousness to shape what spews out, the mind must try then to make sense of whatever emerges: dreams, projections, hybrids, mutated beings.

In Gabriel García Márquez's story "A Very Old Man with Enormous Wings," heavy rains wash a creature ashore and into the courtyard of a young couple. He's a drenched and pitiful man who huddles in a corner, trying to get comfortable in spite of the enormous wings that sprout from his back. Is he an angel or a castaway? When the couple questions him, his answers are incomprehensible. When the villagers appear, they demand to know what he is; his muttered, indifferent responses lead them to torment him, pull out his feathers, burn him with a branding iron. He backs away in his chicken coop, befuddled and withdrawn.

Though the villagers want to know what to call him, what category to put him in, nobody needs to ask how he got there. Oddities, after all, wash up from the sea all the time. Neither does anybody need to ask how he happened to have wings, whether he sprouted them slowly, if it took years of rubbing his back against a barn wall until the nubs appeared. Márquez and the villagers understand that most mythological transformations don't require the passage of time. They also understand, as do the merman's captors, that instant metamorphosis carries with it the possibility of magical wisdom. Winged and fish-tailed men wash ashore, UFOs descend to Orford Ness, and even though we're afraid, we long

to know what they know. Speak to us, we plead. *Say something.*
I know those fantasies, that wish for some benevolent mandate
to revolutionize me, cause me to wake up in the morning kinder,
smarter, more determined to fight for justice. If only we could do it
that way — hear a magical cure, sprout wings, slit open the necessary gills, grow a new face, eat a little kryptonite, whatever it takes
to suddenly become more than merely human.

And this, I finally see, is how the merman's story instructs.
They're out there at sea; the deck is salt-sprayed and slippery.
Home is elsewhere, and up onto the stern of the boat they haul
a figure that has slipped through the censoring nets of their own
minds and silenced their chatter. They stand around and stare at
the chance to change their lives and they refuse it. Back on shore,
the villagers refuse it. In the Márquez story, they refuse it. They
become worse than they were: they burn and scare.

No wonder the force of mythology and art and the Rilke line
in which he declares that in the face of Apollo's headless torso,
"You must change your life." What frightens us might also have
the power to transform us — aliens from underwater, outer space,
some other sky — though we'd be wise never to count on those.
Beauty can do it too, serve as a kind of merman for the soul.
Whether we find it on our deck, on the page, in the garden, or on
a gallery wall, we can be moved by it, stunned by how it disallows
any wallowing or delay. Now? we want to ask. You mean I must
change my life *right now*? Rilke's answer seems clear — *right now.*

Could I do it? Would I even recognize a merman at my feet?
The men testing the trigger device might have been able to call
out a number, a shock rating, a temperature drop, a specific point
at which the trigger fired, but most likely for most of us there is
no single igniting spark. If ever I've been able to measure any real
catalyst in my life, it's been in retrospect: months later, years, even,
understanding the significance of a certain encounter with someone or a night of looking up at the stars. And even if I'd felt the
trigger point approach, I'm not sure I'd be brave enough to allow

the explosion to occur. Mythological transformations, after all, occur in an instant. There's no time for second thoughts, a careful reconsideration, no chance to sculpt the chimera that bursts forth, no guarantees at all. You get whatever hodgepodge emerges — fins, wings, a tail.

I blur my eyes and the shingle stretches out before me, acres of stone-nubby carpet unrolled for miles beside a gray sea that reminds me I love myths of transformation because in reality human change is often so difficult. Incremental, tedious, the result of years and years of a dailiness that abrades and polishes, slowly changes our shapes. Dreams get fragmented, washed away, new foundations deposited. Not one of us wakes up one morning as an angel or a merman. Instead, we shift a little here, a little there. Perhaps the most we can hope for is the transformative power of beauty or love. Meanwhile, we mostly go on, accumulating and discarding what we can. Debris piles up. We ignore it or, given luck, patience, and a trace of consciousness, we sculpt it into something useful, know ourselves to be a tad angelic one day, a little fishy the next.

I unblur my eyes and look down. Underfoot is a bean-sized, putty-colored pebble with deep mauve blotches that look exactly like fish. And next to it, a stone inlaid with something resembling bone, and then a small potato stained with a topographical map of Asia. Here on this stretch of the literal shingle, gravel bits aren't separated from stones, and so the sea pea won't survive. But if this were a shingle in some myth, we humans might. Maybe if we're willing to see — but not segregate — the coarse from the fine, we might even do more than survive. Maybe if every distinction we make between freak and human were tempered by uncertainty, then we might begin to change our lives. Faced with the winged and fishy, the buggy and scaled inside us all, we might find a way to be less monstrous.

The merman never spoke. Neither did the very old man with enormous wings, nor, as far as we know, did anything from outer space. Whatever the Cobra Mist radar was trying to hear remained out of earshot, obstructed by some mysterious noise. No blazing message, no commandment to alter our ways, no explosion that means we must revise our lives. The sky is lighter now, the drizzle has stopped. I'm aware if I don't head back to the landing jetty soon, the warden will be out in his jeep looking for me. I don't want that, don't want the jeep with its fumes and him with his concern, nor do I wish yet to leave this shingle, which seems even larger now than a giant's Zen garden and looks, in fact, stable, as if it's been here, like this, forever. But I know that's an illusion, that even as I walk here, it's graveling its slow way down the coast, inching southward with its litter of iron scraps, blocks of wood and remnants of war, its lore of mermen and UFOs, top secret radar projects and trigger testing. By my left foot, the tiny white tendril of a sea pea twines down between the finer stones in search of a smidgen of nutrition. In the five hundred years since that early map, the nose that is Orford Ness has moved south a couple of miles, its tip now pointed a little more downward. If it were possible to film this drifting debris over hundreds of years and speed the action up, we'd see a nose held high begin to lower, as if the head it's attached to has grown sleepy, begun to nod off.

15 PURPLE SAILORS
The Shape of Chance

> Walk slowly now, small soul, by the edge
> of the water. Choose carefully
> all you are going to lose, though any of it would do.
> — JANE HIRSHFIELD

THERE'S NOTHING ROYAL OR BRAVE or beautiful about dead purple sailors. What's left of their bodies resembles jelly — boysenberry or plum — smeared into sand. What's left of their sails crinkles underfoot like dried bits of cellophane.

It's springtime. I'm walking just north of Mendocino, California, along a coast that my father, who'd sailed for years, had never reached. Neither had I, though now that I'm here I find myself less taken by the panorama than by the wreckage of purple sailors underfoot.

What has caused an ordinary beach to be so fouled by decay that I want to hold my nose? And to be so littered by ethereal wing-like things I can imagine them as intricate mobiles swaying over my granddaughter's crib? No masts or bowsprits, no washed-up captain's log with warnings of inclement weather. Just thousands of these purple sailors in various states of putrefaction, blown ashore by winds for which they had no strategy. I can't call their deaths a surprise. They have a simple design flaw, the kind that keeps me alert to those inflexible habits of my own that I'd much rather deny.

Also known as by-the-wind sailors, *Velella velella* are jellyfish-like creatures of the phylum Cnidaria — stinging animals. But it's their sail that interests me, this now-dried bit I pick up and rub between my fingers. It feels like a cross between papyrus and plastic film. On a live purple sailor, the flap of cartilage, upright on the flattened oval body, acts like a rigid mainsail, propelling the animal far out at sea where it spends its days miles from beachcombers and surfboards, dining on fish eggs and plankton.

Picture the scene from the air: a flotilla of purple sailors so large and color-soaked it's been reported as a blue-tinged oil slick headed, say, west. Now picture another flotilla sailing east. Picture, too, the winds when they begin to shift, redirecting the fleets, which might then intersect, begin to mingle. I like to imagine, even momentarily, the gathering as symbolic: two flotillas convening in the middle of the Pacific Ocean. Were I there to witness such convergence, I might try to spin it into legend — east meets west or two halves of a divided species reunited at last in the hydrozoan Pacific Ocean version of Atlantis, as if some mythic purpose could both explain and redeem what appears to be the faulty design of an inflexible sail. Nothing, however, has ever spawned such a legend.

Making it even more impossible, of course, is this: a purple sailor cannot be counted on. It lives its whole life at the mercy of the wind. When the wind shifts, it shifts. It has no rudder, no swinging boom, no way of turning hard-a-lee, of tacking closer to the wind to keep away from land. Imagine, then, the offshore flotillas starting to lose way, hesitate, their clear sails and purple bodies milling about in the uncertain breeze, a high seas ruffle of chaos and papery collisions. And then as the winds settle down to blow steady, say, from the west or northwest, the flotilla would pivot east, the wind blowing now to gust or gale, the swarm of purple sailors, unable to furl a jib or lower a sail, running helplessly before the wind and bearing down on the shore.

To run aground is every sailor's humiliation, a sign of misreading the chart, the current, the wind, or, perhaps most egregiously, the depth of your own hull. I remember sailing with my father once when the keel thudded hard against the bottom and our forward motion abruptly halted. As the boat tilted awkwardly, wedged in a sandbar, we hoped no other ship would cruise by before the tide returned and we could slink off to some deep-water cove. Did we later review what had happened? Try to pinpoint our miscalculation?

My father was the problem solver; he looked for a reasonable cause and made sure he fixed it. I, however, was in my mystical stage, less concerned with faulty depth finders or outdated charts than with the way I might find spiritual, perhaps paradoxical, significance in "being grounded." For both of us, a matter of control. Neither of us would ever have mentioned shame.

No possibility, of course, of embarrassment in these brainless Jell-O things that lie grounded at my feet. No point, either, in waiting for the tide or another change in wind. Their bodies are 99 percent water. Pulverized by sand and surf, the gelatinous ovals collapse like punctured water balloons. They decompose quickly, evaporate into sand.

If they had been any sailor but the kind they are, they might have been able to jettison the sail while still out at sea. Seamen in a storm have been known to do just that — cut the halyard or the sheet of a mainsail they couldn't lower to the deck. Probably as many died as survived, but who among us hasn't done something similar: chosen between two wretched alternatives because we couldn't help but believe our choices might matter? Even when it became clear that my father was facing his final, unfixable problem, he believed he had options and exhausted them all — radiation, chemotherapy, prayer.

With the toe of my sneaker, I nudge the remains. The degree of decay suggests it must have been yesterday, maybe the day before, when they came ashore. The color has begun to fade. What remains most intact are the sails, which have at last detached from the bodies. They blow around in the sand like crinkly goose down, triangular reminders that biology and the vagaries of wind are the fate of creatures like these. It's tempting to think our fates are never so capriciously determined.

16 ANGEL WINGS
Missing Pieces

There is no mystery in art. Do the things you can
see, they will show you what you cannot see.
— ISAK DINESEN

When the shell of an angel wing clam washes ashore, it's almost always unhinged and broken. Digging in the weedy wrack line rarely
yields the other half. This absence used to matter. As a child, I
hunted for the missing pieces, wanted to glue them back together
and set them upright on the beach, along with other pairs. I fan-
tasized about whole dioramas of wings in the sand, hymns and
hallelujahs, all of them poised at the edge of the world for ascendancy into some other realm that might finally feel like home. That
the waters off Cape Cod failed to deliver two matching wings did
nothing to diminish my vision; it merely meant I wasn't worthy,
too tainted by misdeeds — I was selfish and lazy, I lied — to take
part in such communion. Sometimes I vowed to be better.

But the life of an angel wing clam, it turns out, has nothing
to do with reform. In fact, its shell, too delicate to survive the
grinding surf and probe of gull beaks, requires not ascendancy,
but the opposite: descent into cushiony mud. As a juvenile, the
clam is compelled to retreat to the ocean bottom where it experi-
ments with the first press of its raspy shell edge against the floor,
which begins to split open. Holding on to the bottom with its one
muscular foot, it rocks the front edge of its shell into the crack,

shooting streams of water into the burrow to blast out debris. The slit deepens; the clam wriggles down.

On any beach from Cape Cod to Brazil on a hot summer day, the blue sky above, I can picture thousands of us wading in, while under our bare feet, beneath all that seawater and clay bottom, a last gleam of white disappears as hundreds of *Cyrtopleura costata* — unbroken and with no instinct to fly — fold their wings and sink into the obliterating mud. Even after they've vanished beneath the ocean floor, the clams continue to rock and rasp and bore until they're two or three feet deep — mud below and above, mud all around for the rest of their lives. Maybe the most they can do is siphon a little more algae-laden water into their bodies, burrow in even deeper, until they die and their foot muscles relax, the equivalent of toes uncurling in the deep hard sand. Only then do the clams — unable to do anything to prevent their shells from being shattered or shoved by currents or predators — rise through the mud and into the waves of watery light and buoyancy.

That they finally ascend to a brighter world might have once tempted me toward metaphors for wholeness or heaven. But those childhood illusions have waned, as have most of my worries about missing halves and my own inadequacies. No longer is it the shell's perfection I wish for, or any perfection, really, especially if it insinuates a home beyond this one. That, too, seems to matter less these days.

Now here on the beach after so many years: another half of an angel wing shell — seven inches long, chinalike, curved with a jagged edge. I turn it over in my hands and there are the ribs I remember, radiating from a point where I can still imagine the hinge to the other side and the attachment to some flying creature's back. And, in spite of myself, I feel again my old inclinations, though not for long. I'll not attempt to make much of a dead clam's ascendancy, except to offer it as further evidence that the world is full of both beauty and breakage. If there's an illusionless behest on the beach today, it's this: how to live well, here, among the delicacies and ruins, the necessary insufficiencies of mystery and loss. Things hide in the mud; they rise in the water, and at this moment a pure white shell lies emptied and split in the palm of my hand. That's plenty, if not quite enough.

17 DRIFTWOOD
A Meditation on Soul

> Let it drift
> Down to: elegance and simplicity.
> — A. R. AMMONS

1

Three months after my mother died, I'm back on an Alaskan shore, studying a small piece of driftwood, wondering if it might help me think about the soul, which none of us can say for sure exists. I don't know what kind of tree this chunk fell from. It would have been an indistinguishable part of a high forest canopy, one of a thousand barely visible branches holding the green up to the sun, just another source of low groans in a windstorm.

If I'd been there the moment it dropped, I could have picked it up from the bank of the Taku River and studied the bark, counted the needles. I might have been able to say that it's spruce or fir, to point up at the specific tree. Like so many things, it's most visible just after it's broken.

Since then, it's been cleansed and smoothed by water, scoured by sand, baked gray beyond recognition.

2

Ammons was speaking about garbage when he said "Let it drift / Down to: elegance and simplicity." But he might have been speaking about driftwood as well. Isn't that what we think we see when we decide to bring it home? Simple forms and graceful, unadulterated lines.

3

Even driftwood twisted into wooden ghosts, overgrown worms, gnarled and craggy, appeals. The final arbitrator of its form has been friction with the world. It becomes what it is through long travel.

4

At home I cut it open with a hacksaw. Driftwood doesn't shatter or bleed, wither or deflate. The inside looks like dried marrow, like the interior of a deer femur found after a long winter. It's softer than I imagined. I can push the tip of a pen between its fibers.

5

Driftwood's other possible fate: it doesn't dry out on the beach but stays at sea and absorbs too much of its surroundings. Water leaks into its cells; its fibers grow mushy and bloated. It turns dark and soft. Gribbles and shipworms settle in; fish and birds nibble and pluck. It becomes a floating restaurant, rich in nutrients, home, thousands of years ago, to an ancient crinoid — sea lily — a marine animal that attached itself to the log as if it had a grappling hook.

Soon or later, however, wood bloats too much to float and begins to list in the water. In the case of the crinoids' home, I don't know how long it took, whether the wood hovered awhile just under the surface and sank all at once, or whether months went by while it drifted half upended. And whether the sea lilies, sensing doom, managed to unhook themselves and move to the higher end where they clustered like some sea star version of the *Titanic* before the whole raft went down. Fossils suggest a lot of the lilies went under too, their calcium carbonate scales collapsing within hours as the wood settled heavily on the bottom of the ocean.

6

Gathering fuel on the shores of Kodiak Island, ancient Alutiiq families tapped beached driftwood with a rock. Even children learned to distinguish between the sodden thud of waterlogged wood and a dry thump that resonates through the length of the log. For them, such alertness could mean the difference between staying alive and freezing to death.

7

For those of us who worry about our souls, alertness can be a lifesaver too, though I wonder if anyone can teach us to recognize the last gasp of a soul, our own *cri de coeur*. Whether it's evoked by love or the sea, even a parent's amateur paintings, can we hear it before it dries up or drowns? I'd like to think so. But even if we could, we might, by then, be so far from where we started we'd make the mistake of trying to return. Such a mistake, I'd also like to think, could be, against all odds, a soul's way of beginning again to stir.

18 BITS OF CLAY, GLASS, WOOD

The Strange Attractor

To find my home in one sentence,
concise, as if hammered in metal.

— CZESLAW MILOSZ

OFFERED A TWO-WEEK GIG as a visiting writer at the Haystack Mountain School of Crafts in Maine, I accepted, initially, with the thought of walking on the coast every day for two weeks straight. But, like so many unexpected swerves in attention, I find myself more interested now in the studios than the seaweed. It started almost immediately. I arrived on a cold and rainy Saturday afternoon when the Haystack campus was deserted, the students still twenty-four hours away. Dumping my gear in my cabin, I went immediately to poke among the rocks at low tide. The water sloshed quietly, dimpled by rain. No wind, no waves, and the wrack line — a few shells and sea colander — seemed inert. I turned over some pebbles; nothing scuttled or leaped.

Up the hill, I prowled though vacant studios where the tools hung neatly — chisels, irons, drills, scissors, shears. The machines — rolling mills, beaters, band-saws — were quiet, the work tables wiped and empty except for the stools stacked on them upside down, legs poking up in the air, the floors beneath swept and scrubbed. Everything seemed poised and still.

Just downhill from the glass studio a boulder left behind by a glacier more than ten thousand years ago tilts toward the sea, as if it might, at any moment, begin to roll. It's about sixteen by twenty feet, larger than my cabin just across the dirt road, larger than Thoreau's at Walden Pond. At one time it was molten magma deep under the crust of the earth. Today it's a massive hunk of feldspar and quartz, roofed with ferns, sided with lichen and moss, and a clear reminder of a childhood fantasy.

When I was nine or ten, I used to walk in the woods behind our suburban home and pretend I'd been forced to find a place to live outdoors. In the hills beyond backyards, I'd search out small stony overhangs, woody thickets, protected shelters under rocks. I loved hunting in the underbrush or just below a low ridge, weighing the proper size of one nook against the degree of seclusion of another. My brother, who became an architect, never understood this impulse. He'd be out in the garage, sawing two-by-fours, making little forts out of ladders and leftover plywood. He was the maker; I was the finder. I was reminded of that difference between us as I circled that boulder, one of the biggest at Haystack, and felt the old urge kick in again: yes, there, on the east side, a space I could crawl into where the boulder doesn't sit quite squat on the ground. It'd be a snug home, protected and private, even as it provided good visibility. From there I could watch the woodworkers, the potters at the kiln, even the crew on the kitchen deck. I bent down under the coolness of ancient granite and considered crawling in.

Now, just forty-eight hours later, I'm drawn instead to the sound of concentration — ping and tap, fire roar and clay slap, hammer and beat — and the sight of the inchoate — plops of clay, nondescript tatters of metal, blank canvases, a furnace with a fire and something hot inside. What are all these people actually *doing*?

On the opening night, I make a general request to students and faculty: send me lists of verbs associated with your craft. I want to see whether studying them might help me to differentiate *find* from *make* and to speculate about what happens in the time between them.

The next morning I wander around and watch. Everyone around me is busy, making things. In the pottery studio, Lisa leans over the spinning clay between her knees, an unformed lump that, flung by centrifugal force, wants to fly outward, splatter. She presses slightly in, as if trying to keep something wild and whirling contained, held. In the glass studio, Katherine quickly bends to put her mouth on a blowpipe from which droops a wobble of cooling molten glass. In the metal studio, flame softens a piece of metal and Michael lifts a hammer, ready to tap. There is everywhere the sense of work, of taking one thing and making it into something else, so much diligence that my own impulse to crawl under the boulder seems lazy by comparison. Milosz's statement — "To find my home in one sentence, concise, as if hammered in metal" — becomes a more enticing enigma. What does he mean by *find*? Detect? Recognize? Discover? Is he suggesting the uncovering of something pre-existing? And if *find* is indeed the right word, then how to make sense of the metaphor *as if hammered in metal,* when metal-working is so clearly an act of *making*?

The words begin arriving the next morning, some on a single list from a studio, others on torn bits of paper: *spin* and *smock, planish* and *beat, carve, chisel,* and *hackle flax.* Back in my cabin, I pore over the lists. I don't know some of these words, but they all conjure up images of hands operating tools, fingers doing intricate things with metals and bead and basswood, reshaping raw materials. Clearly they are *making.* Or they're *r*emaking, transforming. But when does *finding* enter the act of making? And must it?

One morning I visit the studios, notebook in hand, and imagine all the participants as mimes. I mentally erase their tools and materials, take away their speech, their tables and stools, dress them in black leotards so I can watch what their bodies do without props. So unlike a mime-as-writer, hunched over a desk with only fingers in motion, those bodies lift invisible objects, roll them over, bend over unseen wheels, cup their fists to their mouths and blow out puffs of air. Their hands twist and swoop, fold and open. In the paper studio, they beat large things. Everyone seems to be kneading, cutting or rolling, stirring the air.

They look like magicians, and suddenly *craft* became *crafty* and I see how *tricky* can lighten into *whimsy,* which, I realize, has kept me dancing around the real question: Can we *ever* know what mysterious force enters the studio of the skilled and turns the simple wish to create into craft and then craft into art?

Even larger: can we ever know what compels our obsessions, what, if anything, binds the disparate urges we do or do not yield to? I'm a woman at midlife spending weeks at a time picking up pieces of wrack lines. Do my gestures imply some still-hidden coherence? Or am I simply a beachcomber without a plan?

Later, Michael tries to teach me how to work a piece of metal. It lies rigid under my hammer like, well, like a piece of metal. How do they get it to curl like plastic? I tap and tap and the thing pings, then dents. Next to me, Michael's hammer taps and taps and the metal begins to bend, stretch sideways in a graceful arch. In the glass studio, I watch the glob at the end of Katherine's blowpipe swell, change shape, its curves grow more elongated. In the clay studio, Bunzy pushes her fingers into the center of a hunk of clay, makes it open like a lily.

I ask for more verbs: *cooch,* they offer, as in *we want our felts wet when we cooch on them.* Or *warp.* They stop me on the deck outside the dining hall: *slap it down* or *jack and crack. Paddle, strip,* or *blow* and, most suggestive of all: *put it in the glory hole.* Eros, it seems clear, plays some role in the creative process. There's intimacy here, a feeling of being drawn to one's materials or perhaps to a certain shape, a love of touching what one works with.

In an essay on resistance, Barry Lopez describes musicians and circus artists as people "who were after some erotic moment in which sensitivity and action fit perfectly together." I might have plenty of action in the metal studio, a busy wrist and forearm and hand clenched tight around a tool, but I have no sensitivity to metal. I don't know how brass might be altered, what kind of pressure makes it move in what kinds of ways. I don't even know how brass becomes brass, what elements below the surface of the earth have combined, grown hot then cold, been twisted and compressed to form that bit of metal that won't change shape beneath my hammer blows. I just bang it blindly.

Sensitivity is a kind of listening, an alertness to both one's aspirations and materials — stone, clay, bits of wood. No writer, for example, can afford to be oblivious to the nuances of the language he or she uses. Likewise, potters have to pay attention to their clay, furniture makers to the nature of oak, metal artists to copper and gold. Is this the beginning of *finding*? Maybe *seeing* is the better word, as in to see what one is working with, to know the properties of one's raw material. The beginner, with luck, bangs a little less blindly each day. He or she has a greater sense of what the material might yield and of some governing design. Somewhere between the two is, perhaps, where discovery resides.

A few days after my ineptness in the metal studio, I wander around on the shore, kick up strands of kelp, and think about the movie *Dirty Dancing*. I especially love the scenes in that movie in which Jennifer Grey is learning to dance. Early on, she has no idea where to put her feet, her hands, how to keep her shoulders down, her chin up. She has no sense of boundaries, what's his dance space and what's hers. She's trying to count and memorize, anything to override or perhaps disguise the giddiness she feels in the presence of Patrick Swayze, who insists, of course, that she look directly into his eyes as they dance.

In the movie, Swayze, making a last-ditch effort just before their scheduled performance, whisks Jennifer Grey out into the countryside, to a stream with an old log crossing it. And it's there, teetering above the water on a six-inch-wide plank, that she suddenly gets it. The large sky — infinite choices — is above them, but the plank is a constraint and the water beneath is a consequence. Their options have been narrowed. It's here that she finally learns something about fluidity and control, the need to balance on the line between expanse and limitations.

I don't know anything about learning to dance. I'm doing well if

I can keep my feet out of the tide. My twin was the graceful dancer with a body like silk scarves and I the one tangled in Tarzan ropes in backyard trees, breaking legs, arms, ribs, and one summer three toes within two days. But I love that *Dirty Dancing* scene for what it suggests about how the movement of the dance might emerge, for how it might illuminate some things about form being the interplay between freedom and constraints.

෴

Back in the metal studio, I study hands. Fingers curl around the handles of hammers, some of them pound or tap. For the more skilled, the motion is rhythmic, light, precise, a repeated pressure banging on the small slips of metal. Other hands hold tongs, dip hot metal into pots of sodium bisulfate. I sketch them with verbal phrases, photograph them, try to memorize their pounding, pouring, turning, burning, slitting, and glazing, and still I can't say what happens in those moments when suddenly a lovely arch emerges from what had been, just seconds ago, a dimpled piece of metal.

Among the craftspeople at Haystack, I can see the apparent belief in the power of a repeated motion, especially in the motion of holding one's material around a spinning center, but I don't see the search for design that's driving it. Is it Platonic? Do you have to have some notion of the ideal before you can fashion the lesser facsimile of it? In the clay studio, Ed closes his eyes, as if to know nothing but the clay whirling between his hands. Up in the glass studio, Will rolls and cradles, his eyes and hands so focused it's as if the rest of us, the studio itself, the granite boulders beyond, have all disappeared. There seems to be nothing in his world at the moment but heat and glass, gravity and centrifugal force. Are they in that state Lopez describes? Alert, sensitive to their material? Perhaps. But that's not enough. Just as I'd needed Annie Dillard and Loren Eiseley when I began to write, so they also must surely have their own version of masters, some notion of form and a standard of excellence that keeps them searching.

In one of our writing sessions, I ask participants to imagine the "hidden studios" at Haystack. They bend over their notebooks and begin to list them: studios high up in the spruces, under the seaside deck, inside people's minds. I list my imaginary below-the-boulder home. Someone describes the space inside a tree, someone else, a secret hut within the kiln. What would go on inside these hidden studios? Not all the work is visible, we conclude; there might be tools all around us that no one can touch, materials that don't appear on purchase orders, work being done beyond our usual awareness. We had begun to speak in metaphor, and I start to wonder whether figurative language is the only way we can talk about the more elusive parts of the creative process. A fiber artist can talk about literally weaving strips of material, but can she talk about the emergence of design? Linda tries: *it's like in cooking, when a sauce starts to thicken.* Or, a jeweler says, *like those Magic 8 Balls you can turn upside down:* at first there's nothing and then you see the future floating slowly to the surface. I think of my private reason for being here — that wrack line down on the shore — and whether its feathery scraps and splintered shells — broken bits of a phantom whole? — add up to anything at all. None of us, it seems, can do it without analogies.

In the midst of the creative process — how broadly am I thinking here? — there must come moments when concentration gets so focused it becomes diffused, and consciousness evaporates. We're magicians stirring an inscrutable pot, and what happens next has little to do with our control. Somehow the clay, the glass, the words, the feet start to move as if on their own. The results may be awkward and sloppy, as things often are until we've paid our dues. And even if we have, we might still be overwhelmed by the surprise of what's happening — on the wheel, the page or dance floor, at the end of the blowpipe or those pivotal moments of our lives — by the way that single coherent gesture seems to appear out of nowhere and makes its own demand.

Back in my cabin, I browse aimlessly through the small pile of books I'd brought for anything that might help me understand that gesture, that complex process of finding the pattern. A book on chaos theory includes a passage on how something called the "strange attractor" controls the movement of something called "boids."

The strange attractor, according to chaos theorists, is the complex and elegant pattern that seems to spontaneously appear: the honeycomb design in silicon oil, tornadoes, schools of fish, the herding behavior of sheep. If I understand it correctly, the strange attractor is both the reason random things self-organize and also the effect. Alone in my cabin, with lists of verbs spread out all around me and the dull hum of the kiln fire in the background, I'm aware how much I love this kind of paradox. It's like an Escher drawing in which up becomes down, one thing becomes its opposite, all in a fluid, turning-back-on-itself movement.

Picture a random bunch of birds pecking away in a cornfield. Suddenly, something signals them and they rise and converge. They form a flock. Something acts on those birds to cause them to congregate, which is the same something that results from their congregating, some mysterious, self-organizing principle that doubles back on itself. *Converge,* it instructs, as if giving marching orders from behind. And even as the birds comply, that same principle, which is also out in front, collects the birds, gathers their otherwise random flights into a perfectly arranged flock that swerves and dips as a single, black-dotted, loosely woven body in the sky.

To study that flocking behavior, researchers have created computer programs in which boids — the term for computer-generated, autonomous, birdlike agents — are set in motion in an onscreen environment filled with obstacles. One book describes a program in which each of the boids was programmed to follow three simple rules about distance, velocity, and centers. The elegant simplicity of demonstration is provocative: the three instructions given to each boid dictated only how it should move in its immediate vicinity — only how to move in the local neighborhood. And what happened, every time the program was run, was that all the boids spontaneously flocked. No matter how dispersed on the computer screen they were when the simulation began, the boids, following only those three rules, quickly gathered themselves into a single flock. No mandate that said, "Form a flock." No directive to follow a lead boid, no instructions to become a particle in a larger unit. The boids had only the rules of "local, boid-to-boid" interaction, and the result was always the coherent and fluid movement of a flock.

What does all this have to do with words or fiber or thread or clay? And even more personally: what does it have to do with jellyfish, shells, driftwood, these seemingly disparate objects I've been compelled to pick up?

What if, I begin to wonder, each boid is a snippet of cloth, mud, molten glass, or language? Picture a whole array of seemingly disconnected fragments strewn around aimlessly. And then we, the makers, begin to listen for rhythms and repetitions and to scrutinize each separate piece even as we nudge them all closer together. As we pay more and more attention to these snippets and how they behave in relation to one another, they begin to cohere, to take on shape, all of it with an underlying rhythm of balance and discovery which then doubles back on itself and becomes not just the resulting coherence but also the organizing principle itself. Form, then, might be the strange attractor, that which both causes things to organize into some pattern and send it flying, and also that which results.

I doubt it can be summoned at will. Its emergence seems to depend on some combination of diligence and luck, of finding and making. It's diligence we have some control over; hence the commitment to keep at it, to keep the hammers pinging, the clay spinning, the glass rolling, the attention focused. The finding, I suspect, is more a matter of letting go and then of alertness, of stepping back and considering what just happened, assessing the effect, then trying to figure out if it's replicable or not, and where to take the work from here.

I haven't yet crawled under that boulder at Haystack. I like the shape and shadow of the nook, the weight above it. I can sit in there, but then what? What would I have done? Perhaps when I was a child to find such a place — to have escaped to my own sense of home — might have sufficed. But though it might motivate, escape doesn't sustain most of us, who must finally learn something about the materials we work with and what we are seeing.

Yes, I love Milosz's notion that a single sentence can feel like home. Whether I've written or read it, such a sentence can feel intuitively right, a kind of return to what I didn't know I knew. But, as Milosz implies, one *finds* — or, maybe more accurately, *arrives in* — such a place by working, by making, by paying attention. No matter what we do — garden or cook, hammer or weave, stack stones or design buildings, as my brother now does — it seems that repeated and intimate attention to our materials is what allows that necessary, mysterious convergence that can lessen the gaps among the far-flung and remind me that connections — invisible and on the verge — might be everywhere around us.

19 SEA STARS
Return

Is that what soul or spirit is, then, the outward-flying attention, the gaze that binds us to the world?

— MARK DOTY

THE SKY IS PINK THIS MORNING and on the shore a whole host of sea stars has been stranded. I know from the charts the moon was full last night, the midnight tide higher than usual. Were the skies clear? Were the stars out? I'd like to have seen these creatures then: stars in the dark overhead and here a spiny constellation draped over the rocks.

One of the largest, a northern sea star, now lies upside down in the palm of my hand. Almost a foot across, its orangey body glistens wet in the dawn light. Hundreds of slender tubes wriggle like antennae, only these aren't sense organs; they're feet, and what they're searching for isn't food or enemy or mate, but something to cling to, any firm surface that can anchor them and end this futile flailing at the air.

Of its five arms, three remain, five or six inches long. I've read that most sea stars lose their limbs to other sea stars' hunger. Traveling in slow-motion swarms, the lead contingent feasts on oysters and clams, depleting the supply for those in the rear, who resort to the nearest neighbor's arm. The epitome of a community food bank — nothing we've come close to. The sea star, of course, can regenerate when the food supply increases and grow back the missing limb, continue unburdened by notions of heroism or sacrifice, even consciousness.

We, in contrast, have to live with those burdens, made heavier by loss and the sensation that often emanates from what's missing. Amputees call it phantom pain, those sensations — tingling or sharp stabs — by which something absent makes its presence known. Even those born without a limb sometimes feel what was never there and experience, physically, what others of us know psychologically — a need to confirm what we feel but can't see.

It's futile to obsess about what's irrevocably gone. Didn't Ahab show me that during that summer of lobster shack and broken oar? But that doesn't mean looking is pointless. But for what, I'm still not sure. Something sacred? Holy? I don't know much about the divine and think of myself as a devout agnostic, in fierce defense of the hesitance that ought to precede a proclamation. My mantra (perhaps too often) is "I don't know yet," though I'm pretty sure solving mysteries is not the answer. *Trying to say what I see* comes closer. How to talk about such things? "*It's as if* . . . is how some of us / have tried to reach it," Stephen Dunn says in his poem "The Lost Thing." *It's as if* a strange attractor is convening random objects. *It's as if* a broken oar has something to say about having the means to get where we're going, about plans we've charted, and what happens when the thing that propels us fails, is nibbled by wood worms and gribbles, and finally washes ashore at our feet.

ॐ

A sea star's motion is slow and laborious. It has no head, and its radial symmetry means it can go in any direction it wants. One of them here has stretched two of its arms along the rock in the direction of the sea. When an arm contacts a hard surface, the star contracts a sac, called the ampula, on each tube and forces water down into the foot, which then expands. Picture a series of squeeze-bulb turkey basters and tiny toilet-bowl plungers on each end: as soon as each foot extends and suction discs touch the rock, the sea star lifts the middle of the disc and creates a vacuum. The disc adheres. When the ampula contract, the tube foot, still suctioned to the rock, is shortened and the rest of the animal's body is pulled toward it. Slowly, it moves forward, a millimeter at a time.

Creeping up on a mussel, the sea star climbs aboard and positions itself, humped up, with some of its arms on one side of the mussel's bivalve shell, the rest on the other. Inside, the mussel, sensing a predator overhead, begins to clench its adductor, that strong muscle that keeps its shell tightly closed and its soft-bodied self safe inside. The tube feet of the sea star — hundreds of them — settle down on the shell, fasten their suction discs, and begin to pull. The mussel's adductor muscle is strong, but the sea star has hundreds of tube feet and can work them in relay fashion, resting some while others continue their steady tug.

To make matters worse for the mussel, the sea star doesn't need to wrench the two halves wide open. All it needs is a tiny gap between the bivalves — even a tenth of a millimeter will do. Once that slit's been made, the sea star turns its own stomach inside out, extends it out its mouth, through the slit, and into the mussel's shell. Digestion begins while the mussel is still in its now-breached haven. Juice dissolves the body, the sea star retrieves its full stomach, and the mussel shell, barely opened, lies emptied.

Fatal for the mussel, ingenious for the star, another inevitable lesson on paradox for us. When its third arm begins to wriggle, I turn the sea star over and carry it back to the water. Oblivious to patience or my unreliable intentions, it knows only the dangers of drying out set against the dangers of being washed out to sea. Try to imagine that twice-daily rhythm, sun on your baking back, your tube feet squishing as you inch along among drying seaweed and barnacles. And then the fierce holding on as the tide comes in above you and wave after wave crashes on top of your delicate tissues.

Look first at the sky, my mother might have warned. *Study the charts,* my father would have countered. Sometimes I wander in art stores, stand behind the shelves and unscrew the caps on oil paint tubes. The smell helps me to conjure her, to place her again in front of an easel and feel Melville's words: *the ungraspable phantom of life.* And sometimes I pull out his nautical charts, pretend that I'm him, plotting his careful course from one island to the next.

Between my competing wishes for mystery and clear-eyed common sense, there's a hum as constant as the tide. It washes over and recedes; it leaves remnants in its wake. Underneath the sea's *come hither* and *beware,* the sand is never the same. The least I can do is keep my eyes open. Attention is what I want to spend. All of it. I don't ever wish to feel inside me a whole storehouse of unused binoculars, magnifying glasses, telescopes.

Were the stars out last night? Silly question, really. They're always out. In the daytime too. Where do we think they'd go? I try to remember this: the obscuring effect of clouds *and* of sunlight, how things that seem to disappear often have not. Up in the daytime sky, the whirling constellations — Cassiopeia, Orion, Big Dipper — may be invisible to us, but stage a noontime solar eclipse and there they are, as always, reminders of other worlds we'll probably never see. And here, underfoot, half a dozen sea stars, about to disappear underwater where they'll go on too, misshapen maybe and less visible, doing what they've always done: making their slow way through a galaxy spread out at our feet.

Foaming and inching its lunar way up the beach, the sea polishes small stones, sloshes into and out of the tiny whorled and bivalved shells somersaulting in the undercurl of its waves. There'll be no wrack line for another few hours, but I'll be back then to walk it again. I take it as a given we can't escape the way the world grinds the living into debris. But before it does, there's a chance for the lucky encounter with someone or something — a painting or poem, a place — that can beckon to what lies broken and hungry inside us all. I believe it's what most of us long for.

Oh Ahab, I often think, if you could have hunted with less vengeance and fewer absolutes, might the whale have someday returned to you what it took so long ago, so violently? Not literally, no leg, of course. Not even in a story would anyone believe a human could do what a sea star can. But something else, something elusive that retreats in the onslaught of high drama and fierce truths, that survives between the layers of the said and the felt, and makes itself known to us only by the ghostly presence of its wanting.